EVIDENCE
&
ADVOCACY

EVIDENCE
&
ADVOCACY

Peter Murphy
and
David Barnard

Published for Temple Lectures
by

Financial Training

First published in Great Britain 1984 by Financial Training Publications Limited, 131 Holland Park Avenue, London W11 4UT

© Peter Murphy and David Barnard, 1984

ISBN: 0 906322 19 7

Typeset by Kerrypress Ltd, Luton
Printed in Great Britain by J.W. Arrowsmith Ltd, Bristol

Contents

Preface

This book is based upon a course for solicitor advocates devised and organised by 'Temple Lectures', which was presented at six centres in England and in Hong Kong during 1982. The authors are grateful to Mr Rowland Ellis for permission to reproduce the material originally delivered at the course.

The idea of the lectures and of this book is to provide a guide to advocates practising in county courts and magistrates courts as to how the rules of evidence are applied in practice.

The authors are separated by six thousand miles of land and water. For that reason each has taken the responsibility of providing part of the book. The major part, which deals in particular with criminal advocacy has been written by Peter Murphy. The chapters on civil evidence and on the presentation of a case at a county court are by David Barnard.

The authors wish to express their gratitude to their publishers for all their help and forebearance. Thanks are also due to Arlene Nabours and Sherry M. Friese who typed the manuscript.

San Francisco   *Peter Murphy*
London   *David Barnard*
June 1984

One

Fundamentals of Evidence

Introduction

This being a book concerned primarily with evidence, and with the relationship of evidence to successful advocacy in the magistrates' and county courts, it must begin by considering what evidence is, and what its function is.

You will not need too much experience as an advocate in any court before you learn an important fact of life, namely that there is a world of difference between having a good case and proving it to a court. A prosecution, defence or civil action may be supported by the facts in every respect, but unless the facts necessary to demonstrate this are both available and properly presented to the court, how is the court to appreciate and act on it? The answer is, of course, that the court can be informed and persuaded only by the presentation of evidence. Evidence may, therefore, be defined as any material which tends to persuade the court of the truth or probability of the facts necessary to sustain the case asserted by the party presenting it. Note the use of the word 'tends'. It serves as a reminder of the sad, but inescapable reality that evidence will succeed in persuading a court only if that evidence appears as truthful, reliable and cogent. Even if a party is in possession of evidence, as it has just been defined, it does not follow that the case will be proved to the satisfaction of the court. Moreover, because the law imposes restrictions on the kinds of evidence that may be adduced, in the interests of fairness to the parties, the evidence must be such that the court is empowered to receive it: it must be both relevant and admissible, when judged by reference to the legal rules of evidence.

Although, therefore, the gulf between having a good case and proving it may be described in terms of having the necessary evidence of the relevant facts, that description raises at least as many problems as it solves. Which of the parties has the burden of proving particular facts to the court, and will therefore fail if those facts cannot be proved? Is there any minimum standard of persuasiveness which that party's evidence must attain, and does that standard vary from case to case? What is meant by relevance? What rules govern the admissibility of evidence? Who has the function of deciding whether evidence is, or is not admissible? Can a party be permitted to adduce admissible evidence which has been obtained in an illegal or unfair manner?

The object of this introductory chapter is to offer some basic answers to such questions, with particular emphasis on the ways in which they are likely to arise in the magistrates' and county courts. An understanding of these basic answers will enable the advocate not only to deal successfully with evidential problems that arise in these courts, but also to develop an organised method of trial preparation based upon the actual evidential demands of the case in hand. This is particularly important for the advocate who has never received a formal course in the law of evidence, or whose training in that subject has been obscured by the mists of time. It is a serious error to try to launch into the detailed rules of evidence without first understanding the fundamental principles upon which they all depend.

It should never be forgotten that evidence has one built-in trap for the advocate which the rules of substantive law or of procedure do not, or at any rate should not, set for him. Almost always, points of law and procedure can be anticipated and researched before going into court. Points of evidence, on the other hand, have a habit of arising quite unexpectedly, because of some unforeseen and often unforeseeable question asked or document produced. An objection must be taken swiftly, or the court will be exposed to evidence which it should not see or hear. Your opponent's objections to your evidence may be equally unanticipated, and if unfounded, must be promptly refuted before the court rules that some vital piece of evidence is inadmissible. A sound working knowledge of the rules of evidence is therefore essential to successful advocacy; you cannot rely entirely on trial preparation, although preparation is certainly necessary to deal properly with all problems which can be foreseen.

Evidence may be presented to a court in various forms. It may be oral evidence given by a witness in court (or the equivalent presented in an affidavit or hearsay statement when permitted), documentary evidence, in which the contents of a document are admitted as evidence in their own right, or so-called real evidence. Real evidence means any material from which the court can draw conclusions by using its own senses, such as the appearance of an object, the demeanour of witnesses, or a photograph, tape recording or film, or a view of the *locus in quo*.

Burden of proof

In both civil and criminal cases, a party who must prove an issue to the court is said to bear the burden of proof on that issue.

In criminal cases, it is a fundamental rule of English law that the prosecution bear the burden of proving the guilt of the defendant. In almost all cases, this means proving all essential elements of the offence charged. This was emphasised by the House of Lords in the landmark decision in *Woolmington* v *DPP* [1]. The defendant was charged with the murder of his wife. His defence was that the gun had gone off accidentally. The jury were directed that, once the prosecution proved that the deceased was killed by the defendant, it was then for the defendant to show that the killing did not amount to murder. Holding this direction to be improper, Viscount Sankey LC said:

> Throughout the web of the English criminal law one golden thread is always to be seen, that it is the duty of the prosecution to prove the prisoner's guilt. . . . If, at the end of and on the whole of the case, there is a reasonable doubt . . . as to whether the prisoner killed the deceased with a malicious intention, the prosecution has not made out the case and the prisoner is entitled to an acquittal. No matter what the charge or where the trial, the principle that the prosecution must prove the guilt of the prisoner is part of the common law of England and no attempt to whittle it down can be entertained.

An essential, if elementary, part of your trial preparation will therefore be to ascertain what the essential elements of a charge are, for this will ordinarily fix the parameters of the burden of proof that lies on the prosecution in your case. Once you have established that the essential elements of a charge of theft are that the defendant (a) dishonestly (b) appropriated (c) property (d) belonging to another (e) with the intention of depriving the other of it permanently, you have identified the facts which the prosecution must prove in order to obtain a conviction. And whether you are prosecuting or defending, you have incidentally focused your mind on the facts to which the evidence must be directed.

It is important to appreciate that the proper time for the bench to assess whether the prosecution have discharged their burden of proof is at the conclusion of the entire case. If the prosecution close their case without adducing any evidence capable of proving an essential element of the offence charged, the bench will uphold a submission of no case to answer, because the burden cannot be discharged. However, provided that the prosecution adduce, with respect to each essential element of the charge, evidence on which the court would be entitled to find such element proved, the case will survive the submission. This is often known as making out a prima facie case. Establishing a prima facie case may not be enough to secure a conviction, because the defence are entitled to argue that the overall burden of proof has not been discharged. The fact that the court may be entitled to find the case proved does not mean that it must do so. Nonetheless, once the prosecution have established a prima facie case, the defence run a serious tactical risk in not calling evidence to rebut it, not because the defendant is called upon to prove his innocence (which would be contrary to the rule in *Woolmington's* case) but because the court may exercise its entitlement to accept the uncontradicted prosecution evidence.

Despite the rule set forth above, and although the prosecution must in all cases prove the guilt of the defendant, there is no rule that the defence cannot be required to bear the burden of proof on individual issues. A number of statutory provisions in fact contain such requirements, which are specifically expressed. For example, the Prevention of Crime Act 1953, s. 1, which deals with offensive weapons, provides that: 'Any person who without lawful authority or reasonable excuse, *the proof whereof shall lie on him*, has with him in any public place any offensive weapon shall be guilty of an offence' (emphasis added).

This does not require a defendant charged with unlawful possession of an offensive weapon to prove his innocence, but only that he had lawful authority or reasonable excuse for the possession, and, of course, the defendant need not prove even this unless and until the prosecution establish a prima facie case that the defendant in fact had such a weapon with him in a public place.

The section cited above is a good illustration of the kinds of case in which a limited burden of proof is placed on the defence. Where the prosecution would otherwise have to prove a negative (for example that the defendant lacked lawful authority or reasonable excuse) or where the burden of proof would be very onerous for the prosecution, but relatively light for the defence (for example that the defendant was a member of an excepted class such as licence-holders) the burden of proof may fairly be placed on the defence on such an issue. In summary cases, this has been elevated into a general principle by what is now s. 101 of the Magistrates' Courts Act 1980, which provides:

> Where the defendant to an information or complaint relies for his defence on any exception, exemption, proviso, excuse or qualification, whether or not it accompanies the description of the offence or matter of complaint in the enactment creating the offence or on which the complaint is founded, the burden of proving the exception, exemption, proviso, excuse or qualification shall be on him; and this notwithstanding that the information or complaint contains an allegation negativing the exception, exemption, proviso, excuse or qualification.

The predecessor of this section was held to reflect and to have enacted a common-law rule, and the principle enshrined in it applies equally to non-statutory offences and to cases tried on indictment: *R* v *Edwards* [2]. However, the rule is of particular importance in relation to regulatory offences in the magistrates' courts, which frequently involve questions of licences or authorisation to perform otherwise proscribed acts. Common examples are a licence to drive a motor vehicle on a road, and authority to possess a dangerous drug.

In civil cases, the party who must prove an issue in order to succeed in establishing his claim or defence bears the burden of proof on that issue. This is a question of law and should be reflected in the pleadings. The plaintiff must prove all the essential elements of his cause of action, and if the defence is confined to a straightforward denial, the plaintiff will bear the burden of proof throughout. However, where the defendant raises an affirmative defence which goes beyond a mere denial, the defendant bears the burden of proving such defence. Thus, in an action for breach of contract, the plaintiff bears the burden of proving both the contract and the breach, and the defendant bears no burden of disproving these; but where the defendant asserts an accord and satisfaction, the defendant bears the burden of proving that defence. Similarly, in an action for negligence, the burden of proving the existence and breach of a duty of care lies on the plaintiff, and the defendant need not disprove them; but where the defendant raises the defence of contributory negligence, he bears the burden of proving such defence. If the pleadings are in order, each party will be found to bear the burden of proof on each positive issue raised for the first time by his pleading, though the true test is the legal composition of the cause of action or defence and not the manner of pleading.

Standard of proof

The standard of proof defines the degree of persuasiveness which a case must attain before a court may convict a defendant or grant relief in respect of a cause of action, as the case may be.

In civil cases, the standard is that of proof on a preponderance of probabilities, which means simply that the party bearing the burden of proof must prove that his case is more likely than not to be true. Any tipping of the scales in his favour, however slight, is enough; but if the probabilities are equal, so that the court is unable to decide between the parties, the asserting party has failed to discharge his burden of proof to the required standard [3]. Where a civil court is considering allegations of fraud or other criminal or quasi-criminal conduct, or of conduct involving a high degree of moral turpitude, the court still applies the standard of the preponderance of probabilities, though in such cases the court may require more cogent evidence, the cogency required increasing with the gravity of the charges, before finding that the scales have been tipped in favour of the asserting party [4].

In criminal cases, the law imposes a higher standard on the prosecution with respect to the issue of guilt. Here, the invariable rule is that the prosecution must prove the guilt of the defendant beyond reasonable doubt, or, to put the same concept in another way, so that the court is sure of guilt. These formulations are merely expressions of the high standard required, which was defined by Denning J in *Miller v Minister of Pensions* [5] as follows:

> It need not reach certainty, but it must carry a high degree of probability. Proof beyond reasonable doubt does not mean proof

beyond the shadow of a doubt. . . . If the evidence is so strong against a man as to leave only a remote possibility in his favour which can be dismissed with the sentence 'of course it is possible, but not in the least probable', the case is proved beyond reasonable doubt, but nothing short of that will suffice.

The law therefore precludes a conviction based on suspicion, mere 'satisfaction' (which implies the civil standard) or even a feeling of being 'fairly sure'. Note, however, that this standard of proof is applicable to the burden on the prosecution of proving the guilt of the defendant. In the cases where the defence bear a limited burden of proof on a specific defence or issue, the standard required of the defence on such limited issue is that on a preponderance of probabilities, and the standard of proof beyond reasonable doubt on the issue of the defendant's guilt is still required of the prosecution in such a case.

Where the admissibility of evidence is an issue, the party asserting admissibility bears the burden of proof. In all instances but one, the standard of proof is that on the preponderance of probabilities, whether the issue arises in a civil or a criminal case. The one exception is that in criminal cases, the prosecution must establish the admissibility of a confession allegedly made by a defendant beyond reasonable doubt—a subject considered further in Chapter 4.

Relevance, admissibility and weight

The terms 'relevance', 'admissibility' and 'weight' are fundamental to an understanding of evidence. The first two refer to qualities which evidence must possess, as a matter of law, before the court will admit and consider it. The third refers to qualities which the court will consider in assessing the cogency of evidence, assuming that it has been found to be admissible.

It is far easier to identify relevant (or irrelevant) evidence than to define it. Probably the most helpful definition given in modern times is that of Lord Simon of Glaisdale in *DPP* v *Kilbourne* [6] that, 'Evidence is relevant if it is logically probative or disprovative of some matter which requires proof'. Obviously, there may be degrees of relevance, and there may be cases in which the same piece of evidence is relevant to more than one fact which requires proof. But at a minimum, evidence must in some way be probative of at least one fact which requires proof. On a charge of exceeding the speed limit, evidence that the defendant's car had defective lights would not be relevant, whereas on a charge of driving with defective lights, its relevance would be obvious. On a charge of driving with excess alcohol, the fact that building tools were found in the defendant's car would be unlikely to be relevant, whereas on a charge of going equipped for burglary, the same evidence might be highly relevant. On either charge, the same evidence might be relevant to the defence. On the first, the defendant might wish to show that he was on his way from work, high above the ground, and had not been drinking. On the second, the defendant's occupation as a builder might offer some reasonable explanation of his possession of the tools which might otherwise appear suspicious.

It not infrequently happens that the relevance of evidence which you wish to adduce is not readily apparent to the court at the moment when you propose to adduce it. This may be because you have not yet called some further evidence, or raised some issue which will make the evidence relevant. The proper course in such a case is to invite the court to admit the evidence conditionally upon your demonstrating its relevance at a later stage. This is sometimes known as admitting the evidence '*de bene esse*'. Be sure, however, that you can fulfil the condition. Failure to do so may result in a successful application by the other side for a retrial, since the court has been exposed to irrelevant and possibly prejudicial evidence.

Although evidence will not be admitted unless it is relevant, it does not follow that all relevant evidence is admissible. In fact, relevant evidence is often excluded because of the rules of law governing admissibility. These rules occupy a substantial part of what follows in this book. They have grown up over some two hundred years in a haphazard and often illogical fashion, and it cannot be pretended that they are either consistent or desirable in all cases. Nonetheless, it is necessary for every advocate to be familiar with them, since they control his or her conduct of every case. The rules are by no means necessarily the same for civil and criminal cases, particularly in the case of the rule against hearsay, which is accorded two separate chapters in this book in order to deal with the radically different principles of law which must be applied in the magistrates' and county courts respectively.

As with relevance, there are cases where the admissibility of evidence has not been demonstrated at the time when you wish to adduce it, for example when cross-examining on a document whose authorship has not been proved. In such a case, the court may admit the evidence *de bene esse*, on the condition that the admissibility of the evidence is later demonstrated. The consequences of failing to comply with the condition are the same.

One of the hazards of the law of evidence is the rule that evidence may be admissible for one purpose, but not for another. There are examples of the rule in this book. Thus, a previous consistent statement admitted for the purpose of rebutting an allegation of recent fabrication is, in a criminal case, admissible evidence that there was no recent fabrication, but it is not admissible to prove that what was previously stated was true. And where the prosecution are permitted to cross-examine the defendant about his previous bad character, because the defendant has made imputations on the character of the prosecution witnesses, the evidence of bad character is evidence of the defendant's credit in making the imputations, but cannot be used as evidence of his guilt. It is important for an advocate to make clear to the court what uses can and cannot legitimately be made of evidence, since practical realities dictate that the court should receive the evidence for the limited purpose for which it is admissible. The court must be prevented, as far as possible, from being prejudiced with respect to issues on which the evidence is inadmissible.

Relevance and admissibility are questions of law, or of mixed law and fact, to be decided by the court before any assessment of the persuasive value of the evidence can arise. This assumes, of course, that the admissibility of the evidence is disputed. In many cases, all parties agree what evidence is admissible or inadmissible, and there is no issue of admissibility for the court to decide, unless the court of its own motion raises such an issue; of course, the court is the final arbiter on any matter of law, and the parties cannot compel the court to accept inadmissible evidence, whatever their agreement.

Assuming that evidence is found to be relevant and admissible, the question of its weight can then be considered. Some advocates make the mistake of considering only whether evidence can be placed before the court at all, and fail to consider its likely persuasive value or lack thereof. Of course, some relevant and admissible evidence is better than none at all and there are cases in which beggars cannot be choosers. But frequently, an advocate can exercise some judgment about evidence, based on its weight, or likely persuasive value.

Evidence which lacks weight is not inadmissible, but the tactical effect of placing it before the court (assuming you have the luxury of choice) can be very serious. The court may well assume that if you are reduced to calling such evidence, your case can have little substance. This is an entirely natural reaction, even if misconceived. If you have one piece of good evidence, of considerable weight, it is generally a sound rule not to dilute it with weak evidence to the same effect. If evidence is weak and unconvincing in your own eyes, it will almost certainly be so in the eyes of the court; if possible, dispense with it and prove the case by other means. The weight of evidence is not always apparent at the outset of a case, and you should always be prepared to re-evaluate it. If the court exhibits great interest in some piece of evidence which you had considered weak, or if some unexpected evidence on the other side demolishes evidence which you had considered to be irrefutable, you must be flexible enough to rethink your approach to the case.

Making and refuting objections to admissibility

Questions of admissibility of evidence are questions of law for the court. This means that in the county court, all such questions are decided by the judge (or registrar if hearing a case as a judge) and that in the magistrates' court, all such questions are decided by the bench, after taking advice from their clerk. The burden of proving that any proferred evidence is admissible lies upon the party tendering that evidence.

In most cases, questions of admissibility can be resolved solely by legal argument. However, in some instances, a question of admissibility may depend upon the court's finding of preliminary facts. Such facts are said to constitute a secondary issue. One example is that of tape recordings. In order for a tape recording to be admissible as a piece of real evidence, it must be shown that the recording is, on the face of it, genuine and original [7]. This can be done by introducing evidence on the secondary issue which shows that the recording is the original, that it has remained in safe custody and has not been tampered with since it was made. Unless the court is satisfied by such secondary evidence, it will hold that the tape recording is inadmissible.

Cases in which secondary evidence is required present some problems both in the magistrates' and county courts. All courts have one or more persons whose function it is to decide questions of law or fact, and who may be referred to as 'tribunals of law' or 'tribunals of fact' respectively. The functions of deciding questions of law and questions of fact may or may not be vested in the same person. In the Crown Court, the tribunals of law and fact are conveniently separated in the persons of the judge and jury, questions of law being for the judge and questions of fact for the jury. Since the judge has the function of deciding questions of admissibility, he also hears the secondary evidence on which such questions depend. The hearing of secondary evidence takes place in the absence of the jury, so that, if the judge rules that the evidence is inadmissible, the jury are not exposed to it and cannot be prejudiced by it. This is known as a 'trial within a trial', and is an invaluable procedure.

Unfortunately, it cannot be duplicated in the county or magistrates' court, because the county court judge, or the magistrates must act both as the tribunal of law and the tribunal of fact. If the court must rule on the question of admissibility, it must in many cases be exposed to the evidence before ruling on its admissibility. If the court then rules the evidence to be inadmissible, it must put the evidence out of its mind. Even in the case of a trained lawyer such as a county court judge or a stipendiary magistrate, this is an extremely difficult process, and advocates tend to be understandably sceptical that it can be done effectively. In the case of a lay bench, it can be said, without in any way criticising lay justices, that the problem is particularly acute.

By far the most critical and by far the most common problems arise in relation to confessions in criminal cases. As will be seen in Chapter 4, the admissibility of a confession depends upon proof by the prosecution that it has been made voluntarily and in the absence of oppressive circumstances, and within the realm of discretion, that it was not made following a breach of the Judges' Rules. These considerations give rise to substantial secondary issues and often hotly contested conflicts of secondary evidence. In many cases, the nature of the confession is such that, if it is held to be inadmissible, an advocate would probably apply to the bench for a retrial before a differently constituted bench because of the likelihood of prejudice arising from the exposure of the bench to it. This is a highly inconvenient and expensive step to take, and is also of doubtful effectiveness, since the bench hearing the retrial would not be bound by the decision of their predecessors. But on the other hand, the trial-within-a-trial procedure has been held to be inappropriate to summary trial, for obvious reasons [8].

So formidable do these difficulties appear that many advocates resign themselves to abandoning questions of admissibility, and confine themselves to attacking the weight of the evidence in question. However, we would suggest that, like any failure to take advantage of legitimate arguments, this is not good advocacy. Not only does a strongly worded argument carry the potential for persuading the bench to exclude, but it also plants a doubt in the mind of the bench as to the weight that ought to be attached to the evidence, even if they decide to admit it. You can follow up on the question of weight in your closing speech, being careful of course to avoid alienating the court by giving the impression of reopening a decided question of admissibility. In many cases, an effective procedure for arguing admissibility can be worked out, and in such cases, the procedure can properly be tailored to the needs of the case.

We suggest the following general approach to arguing questions of admissibility based on secondary evidence in front of a lay bench.

Firstly, always warn the prosecutor in advance that a question of admissibility will arise, and tell him what that question is. In a surprising number of cases, this resolves the problem in itself, because the prosecutor (who may not have considered the point) may agree with you, or at least feel that he can prove the case with other evidence anyway. But apart from this, it is vital to ask the prosecutor not to refer to the disputed evidence in his opening speech, since if he does, your argument about admissibility will lack conviction and may well become wholly academic. No prosecutor should open evidence which he has been told is disputed, and if this occurs, an application for a retrial may succeed.

Secondly, inform the clerk of the general nature of the argument to be presented, and the secondary evidence involved. Try to arrange the presentation of the evidence, in conjunction with the prosecutor and the clerk, in such a way that the detailed substance of the disputed evidence is not revealed to the bench in advance of their ruling, unless absolutely necessary. In some cases, this will be impracticable, since the court's evaluation of the secondary evidence may require a consideration of the disputed evidence itself. For example, you may have to argue that the appearance of a written statement under caution betrays the fact that it is not voluntary. But in many other cases, the bench can decide the matter in the abstract. For example, if the objection is to hearsay, you may be able to say to the bench, 'I apprehend that the witness is about to relate what someone else said to him, and I object that such evidence would be inadmissible as hearsay'. A document may be described to the bench in general terms, sufficiently for them to decide whether it is admissible or inadmissible, and no bench should baulk at this approach if the prosecutor and their clerk have no objection.

Thirdly, make it clear both during cross-examination and in your closing speech that the legal question of admissibility is being raised. Emphasise that the evidence is being challenged not only with respect to its weight, but also to its admissibility, and ask the bench for a specific ruling on this issue. In *F* v *Chief Constable of Kent* [9], it was held that the trial-within-a-trial procedure is inappropriate to summary trial. Therefore, the practice, common in the Crown Court, whereby evidence given in the absence of the jury on the issue of admissibility is later repeated in their presence if the disputed evidence is held to be admissible, should not be adapted for use in the magistrates' court. The practical consequence of this is that your client will not be able to give evidence affecting the issue of admissibility until he gives evidence in support of his own case, after the close of the case for the prosecution. Unless there are very unusual circumstances, it is unlikely that you will succeed in persuading the bench to exclude evidence without hearing evidence from the defendant. Unfortunately, therefore, you will generally be unable to have the evidence excluded at the close of the prosecution case, and will have to make your submission after your client has concluded his evidence, or, if you have no other witnesses, combine it with the other points in your closing speech.

Lastly, as with all legal argument, be familiar with the rules of evidence, and have *Stone's Justices' Manual*, or a textbook on evidence available to support your submissions. You never know when some point will arise which requires you to object, or to resist an objection, without warning.

The procedure recommended above assumes that the objection to the disputed evidence is taken at the usual and natural stage of the trial, that is to say, at the stage when the evidence is about to be given or introduced in the normal course of events. Almost always, this is the correct time for an objection to be made. However, where the evidence is so fundamental to the prosecution case that an opening speech cannot coherently be made, or the case cannot coherently be presented without the disputed evidence, the objection should be resolved at the earliest possible moment. Such a case may arise where the only, or only significant evidence against the defendant consists of a confession whose admissibility is disputed. In such a case, it may be necessary, because of the difficulties identified in *F* v *Chief Constable of Kent*, to allow the prosecution to open the case, but with a statement by both sides about the nature of the dispute as to admissibility. If the question of admissibility cannot be resolved before the defendant gives evidence, the evidence should be placed before the bench with a clear statement by both sides that its admissibility is disputed. Where appropriate, it is proper and responsible for the prosecution to make clear to the bench that, if the evidence is held to be inadmissible, the prosecution case is effectively at an end, and that the prosecution would no longer seek a conviction.

Despite the inherent problems, evidential objections do make for good advocacy in the magistrates' court, inasmuch as any point well taken implies some weakness in the case against you, which will not be overlooked by the court. Often, the seeds of a successful argument on weight are sown in the course of an ostensibly unsuccessful argument on admissibility. Do not throw this weapon away.

Judicial discretion to admit or exclude evidence

The next question is whether the court has any discretion to admit evidence which is technically inadmissible, or to exclude evidence which is technically admissible, in the interests of securing a fair trial. Authority suggests that there is no discretion to admit inadmissible evidence (inclusionary discretion) either in civil or criminal cases. In *Sparks* v *R* [10], the defendant was charged with indecent assault on a small girl, who because of her age, was not called to give evidence. The defendant wished to elicit evidence from the girl's mother that the girl had described her attacker as being coloured, the defendant being white. The Privy Council rejected the argument that the evidence, which was plainly hearsay, should have been admitted despite this. Lord Morris of Borth-y-Gest said:

It was said that it was 'manifestly unjust for the jury to be left throughout the whole trial with the impression that the child could not give any clue to the identity of her assailant'. The cause of justice is, however, best served by adherence to rules which have long been recognised and settled.

As to discretion to exclude technically admissible evidence (exclusionary discretion) the position is somewhat different. In criminal cases tried on indictment, it is now well established that the trial judge has a discretion to exclude admissible prosecution evidence, on the ground that the prejudicial effect of the evidence would be such as to outweigh its true probative or evidential value [11]. To argue for such discretionary exclusion in the course of summary trial involves the same difficulties as does argument on admissibility itself, arising from the dual functions of the bench as the tribunal of law and the tribunal of fact. For these reasons, it has generally been assumed that a magistrates' court should not seek to exercise such discretion. Nonetheless, there would seem to be no reason why the discretion should not be exercised in a proper case, where particularly grave prejudice might arise, even though the advocate must accept that the bench will have to know what it is they are being asked to put out of their minds; although admissibility may be argued without reference to the detailed substance of evidence, discretion cannot be. Cases in which such an argument may arise are:

(a) Where the defendant has become liable to be cross-examined about his bad character, by virtue of s. 1(e) or (f) of the Criminal Evidence Act 1898, there is a discretion to exclude cross-examination altogether, or to limit it to apparently relevant aspects of the defendant's character.

(b) Where the prosecution wish to adduce similar-fact evidence, the court may refuse to admit such evidence.

(c) The court may exclude evidence of other occasions on which the defendant has been instrumental in the handling of stolen goods, or on which he has been convicted of theft or handling stolen goods, where such evidence is admissible under s. 27(3) of the Theft Act 1968.

In civil cases, the position is unclear. Although s. 18(5) of the Civil Evidence Act 1968 provides that nothing in the Act shall prejudice 'any power of a court, in any legal proceedings, to exclude evidence (whether by preventing questions from being put or otherwise) at its discretion', it is uncertain whether any such power exists. As a matter of common sense, the answer is (as it so often is in civil cases tried by a judge) that if a county court judge is minded to exclude evidence in his discretion, he will give it little or no weight anyway, and is therefore likely, if pressed, to admit but then disregard it. To press the judge in such circumstances, when he has made his views on the subject clear, is bad advocacy.

Evidence illegally or unfairly obtained

It is by no means uncommon in criminal cases, and occasionally happens in civil cases, that it will be alleged that evidence, though apparently relevant and admissible, has been obtained by means which are either unlawful or unfair. Such means may range from outright theft to deception, from entrapment to searches made without warrant. In many cases in the past, it was argued that evidence so obtained should be held to be inadmissible for reasons of public policy, or alternatively should be capable of being excluded in the discretion of the court. It is now firmly established that, save in one case, neither argument represents the law of England. It may be that such improper means will subject the obtainer to civil or criminal suit or to internal discipline, but the test is not how the evidence was obtained, but whether it is relevant and admissible. If it is relevant and admissible, the evidence will be admitted, regardless of the manner in which it has been obtained [12]. This does not affect the rule that confessions obtained other than voluntarily or in circumstances of oppression are inadmissible, since the issue there is one of admissibility, not of the means by which the confession was obtained, as such.

The exceptional case referred to above was adumbrated by Warner J in *ITC Film Distributors Ltd* v *Video Exchange Ltd* [13], in which the defendant, who was acting in person during the trial of a suit against him, obtained by a trick papers belonging to the plaintiffs and their solicitors, which had been brought into court for the purposes of the trial. The judge held that the public interest in the administration of justice and the fact that the defendant's conduct probably amounted to a contempt of court, outweighed the defendant's apparent right to introduce into evidence the copies of the documents which he had obtained. The extent of this decision is unclear. In all probability, it is a narrow one based upon very specific facts. Moreover, it should not be interpreted to mean that your documents can be divulged to the other side without loss of the legal professional privilege attaching to them.

Personal knowledge of the court

Every advocate who appears regularly in a local magistrates' or county court is familiar with the flash of recognition that often sweeps across the face of the judge or of a magistrate at the mention of some notorious street or establishment. No magistrate who sits frequently to adjudicate upon road traffic cases or acts of petty theft or violence, and no judge who decides landlord-and-tenant cases and disputes about used cars, can fail to be aware of significant local conditions within his jurisdiction. Moreover, since justices are drawn from many different walks of life, it would be remarkable if, in some cases, magistrates did not possess some personal or professional knowledge of some relevant facts or some speciality such as medicine which in some way bears upon the issues in the case. The question is to what extent the court may make use of such knowledge.

It would obviously be wrong for the court to act on fortuitous personal knowledge to decide a case, instead of relying upon the evidence tendered by the parties. But the court may 'properly and within reasonable limits' make use of such personal knowledge, not as a substitute for the evidence, but to aid it in understanding and evaluating the evidence. In *Ingram* v *Percival* [14], it was held that justices had acted properly in making use of their local knowledge of tidal conditions, and in *Wetherall* v *Harrison* [15] the Divisional Court held that the bench had been entitled to take into account the professional knowledge of one of their number, and to draw on their wartime experience of innoculations, in evaluating medical evidence called for the prosecution.

A good advocate will always sense when a bench is making use of local knowledge, and will try to make that knowledge work for his own case. Such knowledge often aids meritorious arguments, and shortens cases. The bench will often indicate that they are familiar with a relevant geographic area, and this adds a new dimension to a plan or map, or to evidence about the *locus in quo*.

Quite apart from personal knowledge, the court may take judicial notice of any fact which is notorious or beyond reasonable dispute. The taking of judicial notice is a useful device for dispensing with evidence of facts which require no evidence, because they are universally accepted, or nearly so. The device is used by courts more often than the casual observer would suspect. Whenever a court explicitly or tacitly acknowledges that Christmas Day is celebrated on 25 December, or that it is possible to travel from King's Cross to Victoria by Underground, or that the FA Cup Final is played at Wembley Stadium, it is taking judicial notice of those facts, and no evidence is required of them. It is often worth inviting the court expressly to take judicial notice, even where the notoriety of the facts concerned is less obvious than in the examples given.

Notes

1. [1935] AC 462.
2. [1975] QB 27. See also *John* v *Humphreys* [1955] 1 WLR 325.
3. *Miller* v *Minister of Pensions* [1947] 2 All ER 372.
4. *Hornal* v *Neuberger Products Ltd* [1957] 1 QB 247; *Re Dellow's Will Trusts* [1964] 1 WLR 451, 454–5.
5. [1947] 2 All ER 372, 373.
6. [1973] AC 729, 756.
7. *R* v *Robson; R* v *Harris* [1972] 1 WLR 651.
8. *F* v *Chief Constable of Kent* [1982] Crim LR 682.
9. [1982] Crim LR 682.
10. [1964] AC 964.
11. *R* v *List* [1966] 1 WLR 9, 12; *R* v *Sang* [1980] AC 402.
12. *Kuruma, Son of Kaniu* v *R* [1955] AC 197, 203 per Lord Goddard CJ; *R* v *Sang* [1980] AC 402.
13. [1982] Ch 431.
14. [1969] 1 QB 548.
15. [1976] QB 773.

Two

The Rule against Hearsay at Common Law

Introduction

There should probably be an organisation called 'Hearsay Anonymous'. Membership would be open to those judges, practitioners and students (not to mention occasional law teachers) to whom the rule against hearsay has always been an awesome and terrifying mystery. Like its partner in terror, the rule against perpetuities, the rule against hearsay ranks as one of the law's most celebrated nightmares. To many practitioners, it is a dimly remembered vision, which conjures up confused images of complex exceptions and incomprehensible and antiquated cases. When Dickens's Mr Justice Stareleigh refused to permit Sam Weller to relate to the court what the soldier had said, he was merely demonstrating a familiar reflex which had, by Dickens's time, already afflicted lawyers for a century or more and which even today seems to be an integral part of the lawyer's psyche.

'We can't have what Mr X said to you' is one of the most frequently recurring injunctions given to witnesses. It is probably the least understood by witnesses, particularly those witnesses who know Mr X to be an honest and reliable person. It is also, not infrequently, wrong. In fact, you often can, and should have what Mr X said to the witness. If you are conducting a suit for slander or a prosecution for threatening words, and the words spoken by Mr X to the witness happen to be those complained of, you will not get very far unless the witness relates to the court what Mr X told him, and common sense suggests that the words will not be excluded in such a case by a technical rule of evidence. In this instance, common sense is a true guide. Nonetheless, there are many cases where the rule does preclude evidence of what

Mr X said to the witness, and there are even more cases where lawyers wrongly believe it to do so. Never was Professor Cross so perceptive as in his identification of the 'superstitious awe . . . about having any truck with evidence which involves A's telling the court what B said' [1].

It is one of the most abiding and pervasive fallacies to suppose that the rule against hearsay forbids a witness ever to relate what somebody else told him. Close in its scope is the related fallacy that true (inadmissible) hearsay somehow becomes admissible if contained in a document, instead of being imparted by word of mouth. To the destruction of these and other fallacies this chapter is devoted. It should perhaps be entitled 'Everything you always wanted to know about hearsay but were afraid to ask'.

Starting from first principles, the rule against hearsay will be examined in as much detail as is appropriate to practice in the magistrates' and county courts. We hope to make clear that the rule is by no means as difficult as you might have supposed. In fact, if you keep an open mind, you may well end by wondering why you ever thought it was difficult in the first place. The rule is really not that difficult, provided—and it is an important proviso—that you begin by grasping, and never thereafter lose sight of, the definition of hearsay which is considered below.

Before reading any further, please note that in civil cases, the rule against hearsay has been modified fundamentally by statute. It is important to be familiar with the basic rules set forth in this chapter, before going on to study the modern, statutory rules pertaining to hearsay in civil cases which are dealt with in Chapter 3. This chapter will deal with the common-law rule against hearsay as it applies to criminal cases in the magistrates' court. If your problem relates to a civil case in the county court, read this chapter first, but be sure to go on to Chapter 3.

What hearsay is

Hearsay is a kind of evidence which has, since the 18th century, been held to be inadmissible at common law. The rule against hearsay may be stated as follows:

> Evidence by a witness of what another person stated (whether verbally, in writing or otherwise) on a prior occasion is

inadmissible for the purpose of proving that any fact stated by that person on such prior occasion is true.

The same rule applies to statements made on prior occasions by the witness himself, which are generally known as previous consistent, or self-serving statements. However, special rules apply to self-serving statements, which are considered in Chapter 8.

Although this definition would probably not satisfy all academic criticisms that might be made of it, it is a sound one for all practical purposes. Read it a number of times, until you digest and begin to feel comfortable with it. Notice the following essential points; they will be discussed in more detail, but it is worth drawing attention to them straight away:

(a)   The rule excludes evidence of what the witness was told only as evidence of the truth of any fact stated. The rule does not prevent that evidence being given for any other relevant purpose, for example to prove that the words were in fact spoken, or were spoken in a certain way or on a certain occasion. That is why, in a suit for slander or a prosecution for threatening words, it is permissible to introduce evidence of what Mr X said to a witness, in order to show what words Mr X did, in fact, speak.

(b)   A statement was made on a prior occasion if the maker made the statement other than in the course of giving evidence in the proceedings now before the court.

(c)   It is irrelevant whether the statement was made verbally, or in writing or by gesture or by any other medium of communication. The rule is designed to prevent a party from trying to prove the truth or falsity of a fact through the mouth of someone who is not before the court to give evidence and to be cross-examined. It is logical that the rule would also prevent attempts to prove the truth or falsity of the fact by that someone's pen, his camera, his computer, his body or any other means by which he may have expressed himself.

The rule has been explained and justified in a number of ways, some of them related to the historical development of the law. Two simple considerations will suffice here to illustrate the dangers which the rule is perceived to avoid. Firstly, it is impossible to cross-examine a witness effectively on the subject of whether what somebody else stated is true or false. Only when the maker of the statement is before the court as a witness in the instant case will the other side have an opportunity to test what he has stated. Secondly, evidence consisting of a repetition of what someone else has said carries an obvious risk of distortion or inaccuracy (even assuming that the statement is not actually dishonest) which increases in proportion to the number and circumstances of the repetitions made before the statement is relayed to the court. Where a witness tries to repeat a statement which he himself has made on a prior occasion, the basis for the rule is that a 'self-serving' statement has no value when compared to his sworn evidence before the court.

The crucial question: direct evidence or hearsay?

Evidence consisting of the speaking of words or the making of a document, or any other means of communication, may be either direct evidence or hearsay, depending upon the purpose for which a party seeks to introduce it, or in other words, depending upon what the party contends the evidence proves. This concept becomes easier to understand with the aid of a diagram.

Figure 1
       FACT:
  D ROBBED THE BANK .... PW .... HW

Figure 1 illustrates the formation of hearsay. A witness, PW, perceives a fact which will later become relevant to a case, in this instance that D took part in the robbery of a bank. We have called this witness PW as shorthand for 'percipient witness'. Obviously, PW's evidence of what he perceived (in this case, saw) would be admissible, 'direct' evidence of the truth of the fact that D robbed the bank.

But now suppose that PW described to another person, whom we shall call HW as shorthand for 'hearsay witness', what he perceived. It may be that PW did this verbally, by giving HW, a police officer, a description of D at the scene, or it may be that he made a formal written witness statement; it does not matter for present purposes. HW did not perceive the robbery of the bank. He has no knowledge of whether D is the culprit, except in terms of what he has been told by PW.

Next, suppose that because of death, illness, absence abroad or some other cause, PW's admirable direct evidence is not available to the prosecution on the trial of D on a charge of robbery of the bank. Now, the question is: can the prosecution call HW to give evidence that D robbed the bank, based on the information supplied to him by PW? To answer this question, it is necessary to refer to the definition. Was PW's statement made on a prior occasion, i.e., other than while giving evidence in this case? Obviously, yes; it was made at the scene or shortly after the event, and certainly not while PW was a witness at D's trial. Then, what do the prosecution intend to prove by calling HW to give evidence? Again, obviously, there is no relevance in the mere fact that PW made a statement, or in how the statement came to be made. The intent of the prosecution is to prove that what PW told HW is true, that is that D robbed the bank. HW's evidence is, for this purpose, hearsay and inadmissible.

This does not mean that HW could not in any circumstances be permitted to give evidence of what PW told him. It means only that, in any situation where the intent of the party calling HW is to invite the court to infer from HW's evidence that D robbed the bank, HW's evidence cannot be used for that purpose. The party calling HW may not be concerned with the truth or falsehood of what PW said; in fact, whether or not what PW said is true or false may be irrelevant to the case. Obviously, in the prosecution of D for robbing the bank, it is of relevance. But consider now a different set of facts. It has been established that D was not, in fact, involved in the robbery. D has brought an action for defamation against PW for falsely stating to HW that D robbed the bank. The only issue is whether PW did in fact make the statement, or perhaps whether or not he did so under circumstances of qualified privilege. Can D call HW to give evidence of what PW told him? The simplest way to answer this question is to expand Figure 1 into Figure 2.

Figure 2

    FACT 1:
    D ROBBED THE BANK .... PW .... HW

    [FACT 1] .... FACT 2:
                        PW TOLD HW THAT
                        D ROBBED THE BANK ..... HW

From Figure 2 it will be seen that we have not taken an inconsistent position that PW's statement is admissible in one case, but not in another, to prove the same fact. Rather, we have change the fact proposed to be proved. Fact 1 involves the truth or falsity of what PW said. Fact 2, however, involves only the issue of whether or not PW did in fact make that statement, or, if the issue is qualified privilege, whether or not PW made the statement in circumstances entitling him to the benefit of that privilege. Whereas, in the prosecution of D for robbery of the bank, the prosecution set out to prove fact 1, in D's action for defamation, D sets out only to prove fact 2.

Note that we are not saying that hearsay is admissible in one case but not in another. We are saying that PW's statement is hearsay for the purpose of proving fact 1, but not for the purpose of proving fact 2. Why? Simply because the making of a statement may be a fact to be proved, just as robbing a bank may. HW is a percipient witness of the fact that PW made a statement. In order to illustrate this point, consider Figure 3, which shows that, as to the fact that PW made the statement, there is no reason why there should not be a hearsay witness, as well as a percipient witness.

Figure 3

    FACT 1:
    D ROBBED THE BANK .... PW .... HW

    [FACT 1] .... FACT 2:
             PW TOLD HW THAT
             D ROBBED THE BANK ..... HW HW2
                                         (ALIAS PW2)

In Figure 3, you will observe that HW, alias PW2, is a percipient witness of the fact that PW made the statement to HW (fact 2). HW2, a person to whom HW alias PW2 relates what PW told him, is a hearsay witness of both fact 1 and fact 2.

If you now return to our definition of hearsay, which is always the starting-point in considering whether evidence is, or is not, hearsay, you will find that the analysis contained in Figures 1 to 3 satisfies the questions posed when discussing Figure 1. Ask yourself first whether the evidence of HW or HW2 would consist of the repetition of a statement made by PW on a prior occasion, as we have defined that term. Then ask for what purpose the prosecution, or D, propose to tender that evidence to the court.

These hearsay problems are by no means as tricky as they at first appear, especially if you take the trouble to sketch your own diagram as we have done above. A diagram, combined with an application of both questions raised by our definition of hearsay will almost certainly produce the answer. In time, you will find that you no longer need the diagram; indeed, the problem-solving process will probably become automatic.

Distinguishing direct evidence from hearsay: some useful examples

There is no doubt that examples do make the rule against hearsay easier to understand. Now that you have studied the definition of hearsay, you will probably already be recalling examples from your own experience of practice. These will almost certainly include instances where the justices refused to allow you to present some piece of evidence which, at the time, seemed to you to be both relevant and cogent. You may by now have concluded that all concerned were right: you were right to believe that the evidence was relevant and cogent, and the justices were right to rule that it was nonetheless inadmissible. Analysing one or two situations which arise frequently may enable you to foresee such problems in future cases, and perhaps to find alternative ways of proving the same facts.

The following paragraphs discuss five examples, based on frequently recurring fact patterns. Examples 1 and 2 will be examples of pure hearsay, inadmissible on any view. Examples 3 and 4 will be cases where the making of the statement is direct evidence of a relevant fact, and where evidence of the statement is therefore admissible, despite a superficial appearance of hearsay. The fifth example will illustrate a situation in which the same piece of evidence may be admissible for one purpose, in relation to which it is direct evidence, and inadmissible for another purpose, in relation to which it is hearsay.

Example 1: adapted from Jones v Metcalfe [2]   PW, an eyewitness to a road traffic accident, sees the registration number of a vehicle which leaves the scene without stopping, and the bad driving of which is alleged to have caused the accident. PW writes down the number, ABC 123V, on a cigarette packet. Later, he makes a verbal statement to a police officer, HW, and HW writes down PW's statement, including the number, in his notebook. At trial, the issue is the identity of the vehicle, since the defendant, D, while admitting that he is the owner of ABC 123V, states that he was driving elsewhere at the time of the accident. PW is called as a witness for the prosecution. He is asked to state the number of the vehicle in question. By now, some months after the event, PW has forgotten the number, and, since no one asked him to keep it, he has thrown away the cigarette packet. The prosecution wish, therefore, to salvage their case by calling officer HW to state the number as recorded in his notebook. HW's evidence is hearsay and inadmissible, because it consists of a statement made to him by PW other than while giving evidence at the trial, and because the purpose of tendering the evidence is obviously to prove the truth of a relevant fact stated by PW, namely that ABC 123V is in fact the identity of the offending vehicle. The result of all this is that the prosecution are unable to prove the identity of the offending vehicle, and D will leave the court without a stain on his character, a surprised but happy man.

Before leaving this example, consider how easily the prosecution could have avoided this débâcle. If officer HW had ensured that the cigarette packet was preserved, PW would have been permitted to refresh his memory from it while giving evidence, since it is unquestionably a contemporaneous document. Moreover, if officer HW had taken the trouble to have PW read and sign his notebook immediately after it was made, PW could have refreshed his memory from the notebook, since he would have verified it contemporaneously. In these circumstances, there is no question of the cigarette packet or the notebook being introduced into evidence in defiance of the rule against hearsay. All that is happening is that the witness, PW, is refreshing his memory while giving direct, oral evidence of the facts he perceived. This is permissible and usual, and is a courtesy extended to all witnesses. A more detailed treatment of this subject is to be found in Chapter 8.

Example 2: adapted from R v Gibson [3]   D is alleged to have wounded V by throwing a stone at him. At the scene of the offence, an eyewitness, PW, says to the investigating officer, HW: 'The man who threw the stone went into that building'. HW then enters the building indicated by PW, finds D, who is the only occupant, and arrests him. Meanwhile, PW, who has not been asked to remain at the scene, has disappeared and is not available to give evidence at the trial. Again, the prosecution wish to call HW to prove the identity of the offender. Unfortunately, the only way in which HW can do this is to relate to the court what PW said to him. In the absence of evidence of PW's identification, the finding of D in the building is meaningless. HW's evidence of what he was told by PW is, however, hearsay and inadmissible for the same reason as HW's evidence was hearsay and inadmissible in Example 1. Unless D is good enough to admit enough facts to implicate himself, the prosecution are likely to regret their failure to ensure that PW was made available for trial.

Example 3: adapted from R v Chapman [4]   D is charged with driving while the amount of alcohol in his blood exceeded the prescribed limit. The arrest of D for this offence resulted from an accident, in which D was injured. While D was at a hospital being treated for his injuries, a police officer, W, arrived, intending to require D to take a breath test. In order to satisfy a statutory requirement, W asked Dr Z, the physician in charge of the treatment of D whether he (Dr Z) had any objection to W's taking a sample of D's breath. Dr Z indicated that he had no objection. W thereupon administered the test, which proved positive. It has now been established that D's blood-alcohol level exceeded the prescribed limit. At trial, the prosecution wish to prove that the statutory procedure was fully complied with, and call W to state that Dr Z said he had no objection to the administration of the breath test. The defence make the objection that whatever Dr Z may have said to the officer is hearsay and inadmissible. In fact, the evidence is entirely unobjectionable. Of course, it consists of a statement made by Dr Z other than while giving evidence at the trial. But there is no issue of whether or not anything Dr Z said was or was not true. The only issue is: did Dr Z in fact state that he had no objection or not? In other words, the making of the statement is the issue, not the truth or falsehood of any fact stated. As to the issue of whether or not Dr Z did in fact make the statement, W is a percipient witness, since he heard the statement being made. His evidence of the making of the statement is direct evidence, and is admissible to prove that the statutory requirement was complied with.

Example 4: adapted from Subramaniam v Public Prosecutor [5]   D is charged with the unlawful possession of a firearm. He contends that his only reason for possessing the firearm was that he had been threatened with loss of his life by certain criminals, unless he agreed to hide the weapon for them. D relies upon these facts to assert the defence of duress. D wishes to state in evidence that the criminals told him that he would be killed, unless he agreed to hide the firearm. The prosecution object, contending that whatever the criminals may have said to D is hearsay and inadmissible. In fact, the evidence is perfectly admissible. Although it consists of statements made by the criminals on prior occasions, D is not tendering the evidence in order to prove that anything stated by the criminals was true or false, but for the purpose of establishing his state of mind at the time he took possession of the firearm, and thereby also establishing his defence of duress. The issue is whether or not the criminals did, in fact, make the statements attributed to them. As to this issue, D is obviously a percipient witness, having heard the statements being made, and he may therefore give direct, oral evidence of the making of the statements.

Example 5: adapted from R v Willis [6]   D is charged with handling stolen goods. D admits that he received the goods, but contends that (a) the goods in question were not stolen goods, and that (b) even if the goods were stolen, he neither knew nor believed them to be so at the time when he received them. D wishes to give evidence that the person from whom he received the goods had assured him that the goods were not stolen. Is this evidence admissible? These simple facts provide an excellent illustration of the distinction between direct evidence and hearsay, which repays study. The answer is that the evidence of what the supplier of the goods said to D is admissible for one purpose, but not for the other. This means, as a practical matter, that the evidence may be given, but may be considered by the bench only for a limited purpose.

The first question is whether the evidence of what the supplier said on the prior occasion is admissible to prove the first of D's proposed defences, namely that the goods were not stolen. In this case, D is clearly trying to prove that what the supplier said to him was true, i.e., that the goods were not stolen. D is not a percipient witness on the issue of whether the goods were or were not stolen, but is merely relating what the supplier told him. For this purpose, his evidence is hearsay and inadmissible. But for the purposes of D's second defence, the analysis will yield a different result. In order to establish that he was not dishonest, D need not show that the goods were not stolen, merely that he neither knew nor believed that they were stolen, at the time he received them. In other words, just as in example 4, D is seeking to establish his state of mind. His state of mind was governed, at least in part, by what he was told by the supplier of the goods. The supplier's statement is accordingly direct evidence of D's state of mind, and is admissible for that limited purpose, even though it is not admissible on the issue of whether the goods were stolen. D should be permitted to relate what the supplier told him, with a view to showing that he (D) neither knew nor believed the goods to be stolen at the time he received them from the supplier.

When you encounter a hearsay problem in the magistrates' court, you may find it useful to review this part of this chapter, at least until you become more comfortable with the rule. A helpful technique may be to turn first to the definition of hearsay (always the starting-point), secondly to the diagrams (make your own to correspond to the facts of your case) and lastly to the examples, to find one that offers guidance. With experience, you will find that these steps will become routine. As in all fields of study and application, practice makes perfect.

Exceptions to the rule against hearsay

The modern statutory rules which apply to hearsay in civil cases (Chapter 3) are sometimes referred to as constituting an 'exception' to the rule against hearsay. It would be more accurate, however, to describe them as a substitution for the common-law rule against hearsay. In criminal cases, the common-law rule against hearsay, as described above, continues to apply. There are exceptions to the rule in criminal cases, which are exceptions in the true sense, in that they permit hearsay evidence to be admitted in limited circumstances, notwithstanding the general application of the common-law rule. It is these exceptions which will be considered in this chapter. The exceptions applicable to criminal cases have grown up and have been developed by case-law, with little statutory intervention, over a period of some two centuries. It is, therefore, hardly surprising that they appear as a veritable jungle of esoteric rules, most of which lack discernible contemporary meaning. Fortunately, the areas of concern in the magistrates' court are limited, and much of this abstruse learning can be ignored in this book. In fact, we shall confine ourselves to three exceptions which are important and which are relatively easily understood. One of these, which we shall call the 'excited utterance rule' in preference to its mysterious traditional name of the '*res gestae* rule', is concerned with verbal statements. The other two, relating respectively to facts recorded in public documents and in trade or business records, are concerned with documentary hearsay.

These three exceptions have in common that, because they are exceptions to the rule against hearsay, they permit evidence to be admitted which would otherwise be excluded by the rule. It is worth drawing attention to this apparently obvious proposition, in order to emphasise the fact that, when evidence is admitted by virtue of such an exception, the hearsay statement may be regarded by the bench as evidence of the truth of any fact stated therein. In terms of economy of time and effort, this result produces considerable savings by eliminating the need to call witnesses who are often difficult to trace, and whose recollection of the events they recorded in the statement would often be unsatisfactory.

The excited utterance rule

The name which we have adopted for this exception is the American usage. It is vivid and descriptive of the scope of the exception, and is generally more helpful than the traditional common-law appellation of *res gestae*. But to mutilate Shakespeare a little, an exception by any other name would be just as effective. This exception needs no complex description. The exception is simply this: where a person who is involved in or witnesses an event makes an uncalculated, spontaneous statement in the nature of an outburst in the heat of the moment, referring to the event, the statement may be admissible as evidence of the truth of what was stated. The reason for the exception is that such statements explain the event, or lend a significance to it of such magnitude that the true nature and circumstances of the event become clearer.

The statement may be admitted only if it is shown that it was truly spontaneous. The importance of this is that spontaneity tends to negate the possibility of a calculated self-serving declaration by the witness. Almost three centuries of jurisprudence have failed to improve on the formulation of the exception made by Holt CJ in *Thompson* v *Trevanion* in 1693. The plaintiff had sued for an assault on his wife, and the Chief Justice said, 'that what the wife said immediately upon the hurt received, and before that she had time to devise or contrive any thing for her own advantage, might be given in evidence' [7]. A good modern statement of the rule is to be found in the speech of Lord Wilberforce in *Ratten* v *R* [8]. On no account, however, read any 19th-century cases dealing with this exception. The law became extremely artificial and confused during that period.

As Holt CJ rightly pointed out in *Thompson* v *Trevanion*, the immediacy of the statement as a reaction to the event is an indication of its spontaneity. The modern cases recognise that to require literal contemporaneity with the event would be artificial and unduly restrictive (this was the main mistake made during the 19th century). A gap in time, before the event ('Look out! That car is going to hit her!') or after it ('That driver made no attempt to stop at the red light!') is acceptable. In *R* v *Nye and Loan* [9], a statement made by the victim of an assault, in which he identified his assailants to the police, was admitted under this exception, even though several minutes had elapsed since the assault, where the victim had been sitting nearby and recovering during the intervening time.

But you must demonstrate to the bench that the statement was both spontaneous and uncalculated. This may be done by asking the witness to describe how the statement came to be made, and his state of mind at the time. Of course, you should do this before allowing the witness to relate what he said, so that the bench are not exposed to inadmissible evidence, if they decide against you.

Used in the right way, the excited utterance rule can often be employed to put before the court very cogent, contemporaneous statements. It is particularly useful in giving evidence of dramatic incidents, such as a fight or an accident, in which it is likely to be easier to persuade the court that the statement was made in the heat and excitement of the moment. If such a statement is tendered against you, ask the court for permission to cross-examine the witness about its spontaneity, before the detail of the statement is revealed. Ask about the timing, and challenge it, if there is any possibility of concoction.

Facts recorded in public documents

A public document is one that is created and maintained as a public record, for the purpose of future public reference. Such documents were relatively few in the days when this exception was developed at common law, consisting of such things as parish and manorial records. Today, there is a vast and ever-increasing multiplicity of public records, dealing with an almost inconceivable range of subjects. The original reason for the exception, that public records might be admitted as evidence of the truth of facts stated in them, was simply that such documents were presumptively reliable, as having been compiled by a person acting under a public duty, and it was therefore perceived that no reason of policy required their exclusion under the hearsay rule.

Public documents are still admitted on this basis, although it is recognised that public records are now compiled through the efforts of more than one recorder, and may well be maintained by a person who played no part in the compilation at all. The conditions for admissibility of public documents under this rule, which must be demonstrated to the court before the evidence can be admitted, are as follows:

(a)   The document must have been made and preserved for public use, and must contain facts of public interest.

(b)   It must be a record which is open to public inspection.

(c)   The entry in question must have been made promptly after the events which it purports to record or describe.

(d)   The entry in question must have been made by a person who had a duty to inquire into the facts recorded, and to satisfy himself of the truth of such facts.

Whether or not a document contains public, rather than private facts, and whether such facts were promptly recorded, are questions which the bench must decide on a basis of common sense. In almost every case, the answer is apparent, and there are no hard-and-fast rules. These conditions are liberally construed in favour of admissibility in modern times. The fourth condition caused some problems for the Court of Appeal in *R* v *Halpin* [10], where the appellant cogently demonstrated that documents maintained by the Registrar of Companies could not possibly be said to satisfy the condition, because it would be impossible for a public official to satisfy himself of the truth of the facts recorded therein. Recognising that this fact would apply to a large number of modern public documents, the court held that it is sufficient if the duty is shared by two persons, the first having the duty to inquire into and satisfy himself of the truth of facts of public interest and to record such facts in a document, the second having the duty to receive the document and preserve it for future public reference.

In civil cases, the exception has been codified by statute (Civil Evidence Act 1968, s. 9) without any substantive changes. In criminal cases, there may be express statutory provisions which make individual documents admissible quite apart from the common-law public documents exception. The facts of *Halpin* are a good illustration. The Companies Act 1948 provided for the admissibility of certain corporate documents, but not those which the prosecution wished to introduce into evidence. The latter were therefore admissible, if at all, only by virtue of the common-law exception. This shows that the correct approach is to examine the document from both standpoints. Look first for an express statutory provision, which makes the question of admissibility much more straight-forward. Failing this, see whether the conditions of admissibility at common law can be demonstrated.

The categories of public document are almost beyond classification because of their number and variety. They include public registers, surveys, inquisitions, official certificates issued by public officers under authority, many corporate records, and even authoritative published works such as maps and histories.

Trade and business records: the Criminal Evidence Act 1965

In an increasing number of criminal cases, the records kept by businesses provide significant evidence which no court can afford to ignore. Many offences of obtaining by deception, false accounting and the like can be proved only by such evidence. In many other cases, business records play a scarcely less important role. This is only to be expected in a society which seems more and more preoccupied with creating records, and with inventing more and more sophisticated methods of keeping them as time goes by.

It is therefore surprising, except perhaps to anyone familiar with the history of the rule against hearsay, that it took a shattering judgment of the House of Lords in the mid 1960s to demonstrate the complete inadequacy of the common law, as it then stood, to make such records available as admissible evidence in the criminal courts. The decision in question was *Myers* v *DPP* [11], and it is still of great importance because, even though Parliament reacted to it by enacting a statutory provision for the admissibility of trade or business records, the new legislation left untouched other documentary hearsay. Documents outside the scope of the statutory provisions were, and still are, inadmissible unless they can be brought within the scope of some other exception, such as the public documents rule. The case is also another excellent illustration of the rule against hearsay at work.

The appellant was convicted of offences of dishonesty, which consisted of stealing cars, buying up other, wrecked cars, disguising the stolen cars so that they corresponded as nearly as possible with the wrecks and their log-books, and finally selling the stolen cars as if they were the wrecks. The prosecution wished to prove the identity of the stolen cars by introducing evidence that an indelible number had been stamped on the cylinder blocks of the cars at the time of manufacture. This number would unquestionably identify the vehicle in which the cylinder block had originally been installed, and would show that it had since been transposed into a different vehicle. The numbers had originally been recorded on cards by those assembling the cars, and were later transferred to microfilm. The question before the House of Lords was whether these records were admissible. By a majority, the House held that, while it would certainly be both reasonable and convenient that they should be admissible, they were clearly hearsay, fell within no recognised exception and were accordingly inadmissible. Having studied this chapter thus far, you would have reached the same conclusion without difficulty. The House rejected the suggestion that it should create a new common-law exception to the rule against hearsay, holding that so major a departure from the common law should be effected, if at all, by statute.

Parliament, faced with the prospect that prosecutions for many serious offences of dishonesty might well come to an abrupt halt (think of the impossible problems the prosecution would have experienced in *Myers* in attempting to prove the same facts by means of direct oral evidence) responded with the Criminal Evidence Act 1965. Section 1 of the Act provides as follows:

(1)   In any criminal proceedings where direct oral evidence of a fact would be admissible, any statement contained in a document and tending to establish that fact shall, on production of the document, be admissible as evidence of that fact if—

(a)   the document is, or forms part of, a record relating to any trade or business and compiled, in the course of that trade or business, from information supplied (whether directly or indirectly) by persons who have, or may reasonably be supposed to have, personal knowledge of the matters dealt with in the information they supply; and

(b)   the person who supplied the information recorded in the statement in question is dead, or beyond the seas, or unfit by reason of his bodily or mental condition to attend as a witness, or cannot with reasonable diligence be identified or found, or cannot reasonably be expected (having regard to the time which has elapsed since he supplied the information and to all the circumstances) to have any recollection of the matters dealt with in the information supplied. . . .

(4)   In this section 'statement' includes any representation of fact, whether made in words or otherwise, 'document' includes any device by means of which information is recorded or stored and 'business' includes any public transport, public utility or similar undertaking carried on by a local authority and the activities of the Post Office.

Like the common-law exceptions which we have already discussed, the admissibility of the evidence described is made subject to certain conditions. If you wish evidence to be admitted under the section, you must be prepared, if called upon to do so, to show that the conditions are met. If you are trying to keep evidence out, make your opponent demonstrate that the conditions have been fulfilled, before the evidence is tendered to the bench. This can be surprisingly difficult to do, and it is equally surprising how often inadmissible evidence is admitted by default of objection. For a court to admit evidence, purportedly under the Act, without enquiring into and ruling on its admissibility, if invited to do so, is an error of law: see *R* v *Nicholls* [12].

Although the conditions are easy enough to derive from a systematic reading of the section itself, they are also important enough to justify setting them out in order, with brief comments, so as to provide a checklist:

(a)   This Act applies only to criminal proceedings, and to facts of which direct oral evidence would be admissible, i.e., which are not objectionable from an evidential standpoint apart from the rule against hearsay.

(b)   The hearsay statement must be contained in a 'document' (see s. 1(4)), the document must be produced to the court, and the statement must tend to establish the fact, i.e., be relevant in proving the fact.

(c)   The document must be, or form part of a record. This sounds obvious enough, but the Court of Appeal has questioned whether a random or unsystematic collection of documents constitutes a record: *R* v *Tirado* [13]. If you are faced with some collection of documents which has not been compiled so much as allowed to fall into a pile, this can be a useful argument. And it has a guaranteed surprise value: no one ever expects this one.

(d)   The record must relate to a trade or business and have been compiled in the course of that trade or business. Some interesting questions have arisen about the meaning of 'trade or business', which are not solved by the partial definition in s. 1(4). There is still much room for argument in individual cases. The test seems to be that the organisation which spawned the record is acting as a commercial entity, which has been held to exclude such institutions as National Health Service hospitals (though not necessarily private hospitals): *R* v *Crayden* [14]; and a Home Office Supply Department: *R* v *Gwilliam* [15]. That still leaves a lot of doubtful cases out there, and there is still room for argument on many questions. For example, the Bank of England is still of doubtful status for the purposes of this rule.

(e)   There must be proof of actual or supposed personal knowledge of the facts supplied. This can usually be established, or refuted, by an inquiry into the circumstances in which the document came to be made—which is also useful for showing whether it was compiled in the course of the trade or business, another much-over-looked requirement.

(f)   Lastly (and this is a condition ignored with a quite astonishing frequency, given its prominence in the section) it must be demonstrated that oral evidence of the information recorded in the statement is unavailable or useless for at least one of the reasons set forth in s. 1(1)(b). Very often, a party will try to put in the document without even enquiring about the whereabouts, health or recollection of the maker. This is usually a relatively simple fact to establish, and if it can be shown that a live witness could and should be called, the hearsay statement is doomed to exclusion. Of all objections to statements tendered under the Act, this is undoubtedly the most cogent, because no court likes to feel that it is being fobbed off with second-best evidence, when the best could have been produced.

The very frequency with which trade or business records are now used in criminal cases is sufficient reason to study and re-study the Criminal Evidence Act 1965. Day in and day out, documents are put in evidence in magistrates' courts, with a dimly understood reliance on the Act. Most advocates, if they are honest, will recall cases in which they could have objected to some document taken from the records of a trade or business, and cases in which they got in some documents which should probably have been excluded. All of which goes to say that a mastery of this short statutory provision is a valuable weapon in your armoury, whether as prosecutor or defender. Many are the times when it will enable you to gain the initiative by getting in an unexpected piece of evidence, or by keeping out some piece of evidence on which your opponent intended to rely. Underlying it all is the principle that, unless the conditions are fulfilled, the document falls foul of the rule against hearsay, as expounded in *Myers* v *DPP*.

Notes

1. [1965] Crim LR 68, 82.
2. [1967] 1 WLR 1286.
3. (1887) 18 QBD 537.
4. [1969] 2 QB 436.
5. [1956] 1 WLR 965.
6. [1960] 1 WLR 55.
7. (1693) Skin 402.
8. [1972] AC 378.
9. (1977) 66 Cr App R 252.
10. [1975] QB 907.
11. [1965] AC 1001.
12. (1976) 63 Cr App R 187.
13. (1974) 59 Cr App R 80, 89.
14. [1978] 1 WLR 604.
15. [1968] 1 WLR 1839.

Three

The Rule against Hearsay in Civil Cases

Introduction

The hearsay rule operates in criminal cases to prevent evidence which may be logically relevant (and which is sometimes highly relevant) going before the court. Of course, in a criminal trial, the tribunal is normally made up of lay persons, magistrates or a jury, so there is some sense in excluding from their consideration evidence which cannot be tested by cross-examination. In civil cases, however, the issues of fact are decided by a judge, who is well able to make the proper allowance, when giving judgment, for the fact that some of the evidence has not been subjected to cross-examination. For this reason, the rule against hearsay, which plays so large a part in the law of criminal evidence, has been radically modified by statute in civil cases. The nature of this modification may be appreciated by considering an example.

Suppose that an accident has occurred on a motorway leading to a large airport. Your client's car has been damaged in the collision. He has suffered injuries and he has been faced with a very substantial repair bill. The accident was witnessed by two independent people: the first, a Japanese tourist on his way to the airport; the second, an American businessman travelling into the city from the airport. Shortly after the accident, Police Constable A arrived at the scene and made notes of the positions of the vehicles involved and the apparent extent of the damage. The Japanese tourist made an oral statement to Police Constable A, who recorded that statement in his notebook. The American businessman later visited the police station and made a written statement to Police Constable A.

Now, if the facts of this accident were to be examined by the local magistrates' court in the context, for example, of the prosecution of the other driver on a charge of careless driving, it is clear that the prosecution would not be allowed to call Police Constable A to tell the court what the Japanese tourist had said to him, or to put in as part of their evidence the written statement made by the American businessman. This may be demonstrated by using a diagram of the kind employed in Chapter 2.

Figure 1

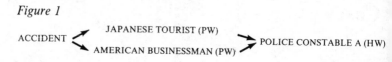

Figure 1 shows that the Japanese tourist and the American businessman are direct or percipient witnesses of the accident. Police Constable A is a direct or percipient witness of the accident, in so far as his evidence of the positions of the vehicles and the apparent damage is concerned, since he perceived these facts. At the same time, Police Constable A is clearly a hearsay witness with respect to the statements made to him by the Japanese tourist and the American businessman. Therefore, in a criminal case, Police Constable A would be permitted to state his observation of vehicle positions and damage, but not what he had been told by the Japanese tourist or the American businessman.

By contrast, when the same facts come to be investigated by the local county court judge, in a civil action brought by your client against the other driver, the position will be very different. Provided you, as the plaintiff's advocate, understand how the hearsay rule has been modified for civil litigation, you will be able to put in front of the court the evidence of those witnesses who are not able to attend and give oral evidence at the trial. This is possible because of the provisions of the Civil Evidence Act 1968. In simple terms, that Act enables the advocate to do two very important things:

(a)   To ask a witness to tell the court what somebody else has told him about the facts.

(b)   To put in front of the court written accounts of the matters in dispute.

In both cases, such evidence is admissible for the purpose of proving the truth of the facts related or contained in the written account.

Before looking at the provisions of the Civil Evidence Act 1968 in more detail, it is worth noting two important points.

Firstly, the act permits hearsay evidence only of facts of which direct oral evidence would be admissible. In other words, evidence which is inadmissible, quite apart from any hearsay considerations, or which comes from an incompetent witness, cannot be admitted in hearsay form any more than it could by way of direct oral evidence.

The second is that the admissibility of hearsay evidence under the Civil Evidence Act 1968 is subject to important procedural rules, which will be considered later in this chapter.

With these points in mind, the most important provisions of the Civil Evidence Act 1968 will now be considered, and for this purpose it will be assumed that the Japanese tourist and the American businessman have returned home to Tokyo and Dallas, respectively, and will not be available for trial. In a criminal case, their absence would pose serious problems for the prosecution, and might even be fatal to the prosecution case. But in the civil action, you are able to take advantage of the 1968 Act to put before the court their accounts of how the accident occurred.

Admissible hearsay statements: Civil Evidence Act 1968, section 2(1)

By s. 2(1) of the Act:

> In any civil proceedings a statement made, whether orally or in a document or otherwise, by any person, whether called as a witness in those proceedings or not, shall, subject to this section and to rules of court, be admissible as evidence of any fact stated therein of which direct oral evidence by him would be admissible.

Since this subsection provides that the statement may have been made 'orally or in a document or otherwise' and 'by any person, whether called as a witness in those proceedings or not', it enables you to put in evidence both the oral statement of the Japanese tourist and the written statement made by the American businessman. Furthermore, the statements are admissible to prove the truth of the facts contained in them. Naturally, you may have to address the judge with regard to the weight to be attached to such statements.

In some cases, the weight to be attached to a hearsay statement may be markedly less than the weight that could be commanded by a witness giving oral evidence. This may be because the statement is not as clear as it might be, or it is untested by cross-examination. Section 6(3) of the Act lays down some common-sense rules about how the question of weight shall be approached, regard must be had to all the circumstances under which the statement was made, for example whether it was made contemporaneously with the facts stated, and whether or not the maker of the statement had any incentive to conceal or misrepresent the facts. In the example, it is difficult to imagine that either witness had any motive for doing this, and provided the statements disclosed that the witnesses had a clear view of the accident, there is no reason why their statements should not command considerable weight.

It should be noted that there is one difference between the oral statement made by the Japanese tourist and the written statement made by the American businessman, not in terms of admissibility, but in terms of how the statement should be proved. Section 2(3) of the Act provides that where the hearsay statement was made otherwise than in a document it may only be proved by a person who heard or otherwise perceived it being made. (There is an exception to this rule where the oral statement was made by a person while giving oral evidence in some other legal proceedings, whether civil or criminal, in which case the statement may be proved in any manner authorised by the court.) In other words, the oral statement of the Japanese tourist may be proved only by the evidence of Police Constable A. If Police Constable A happens to be available at trial, the statement could not be proved, for example, by calling another officer to read the contents of Police Constable A's notebook, or to state that Police Constable A had told him what the Japanese tourist had said.

Section 2 of the Act has one other useful provision. Let us assume that the American businessman happens to be back in England at the time of the trial, and is available to give evidence. Owing to the lapse of time, however, he is unable to recall enough detail of the accident to make his oral evidence really useful. Section 2(2) permits you to introduce his hearsay statement in addition to his oral evidence, subject to leave of the court. Although this may be made the subject of some comment by the other side, it is a proper and worthwhile step to take in any case where a witness is unsure or does not remember. In addition to requiring the leave of the court, s. 2(2) provides that the hearsay statement shall not be given in evidence before the conclusion of the examination-in-chief of the maker of the statement, unless the court permits evidence of the making of the statement to be given by some other witness, or permits the witness to narrate the statement in the course of his evidence in chief, in order to prevent his evidence from being unintelligible without it.

Admissible hearsay records: Civil Evidence Act 1968, section 4

Next, assume that you wish to prove the extent of the damage to your client's car and the repairs that were made necessary because of the collision. Your client was detained in hospital as a result of his injuries, and underwent surgery and prolonged medical treatment. Ordinarily, of course, you would be able to call the mechanic responsible for the repair of the car, but you might not be able to call, or may not want to call, all the doctors and nurses responsible for attending to your client throughout his stay in hospital. If this situation occurred in the context of a criminal case in the magistrates' court, you would probably be able to put the mechanic's time sheets in evidence under the Criminal Evidence Act 1965; if the hospital was a National Health establishment, you would not be able to put in the medical records. In a civil action, however, both would be admissible by virtue of s. 4(1) of the Civil Evidence Act 1968, which provides as follows:

> Without prejudice to section 5 of this Act, in any civil proceedings a statement contained in a document shall, subject to this section and to rules of court, be admissible as evidence of any fact stated therein of which direct oral evidence would be admissible, if the document is, or forms part of, a record compiled by a person acting under a duty from information which was supplied by a person (whether acting under a duty or not) who had, or may reasonably be supposed to have had, personal knowledge of the matters dealt with in that information and which, if not supplied by that person to the compiler of the record directly, was supplied by him to the compiler of the record indirectly through one or more intermediaries each acting under a duty.

In order to introduce this evidence, you must satisfy the requirements set out in the section.

Firstly, the record must be in documentary form, and it must actually constitute a 'record'. There is no statutory definition of what amounts to a record, but it has been defined in one case [1] as follows:

> The intention of that section was, I believe, to admit in evidence records which a historian would regard as original or primary sources, that is, documents which either give effect to a transaction itself or which contain a contemporaneous register of information supplied by those with direct knowledge of the facts.

If the document does not contain all the information supplied, or in some way edits that information, or expresses opinions on the information, it may not amount to a record [2].

Note also that the person who has compiled the record must have been acting under a duty to do so. Section 4(3) defines such duty very widely, and provides that the person may have been acting in the course of any trade, business, profession or other occupation, or for the purposes of any paid or unpaid office held by him. If the compiler of the record obtained his information indirectly, through one or more intermediaries, then those intermediaries must also have been acting under a similar duty.

Finally, the person who supplied the information from which the record was compiled must have had personal knowledge of the matters dealt with in the information, or failing this it must be reasonable to suppose that the supplier had such personal knowledge.

In the light of these provisions, there should be no difficulty in the way of putting into evidence the records of the mechanic and of the hospital. However, one word of caution must be added. While these records are admissible evidence of the facts contained in them, they would not necessarily be admissible evidence of any opinion stated in the records. If you require some medical opinion about your client's past, present or future condition, it would be unsafe to rely solely upon the medical records. Although the Civil Evidence Act 1972 extends the 1968 Act to statements of opinion, it also provides that a statement of opinion contained in a record shall not be admissible unless that statement would be admissible if made in the course of giving oral evidence by the person who originally supplied the information from which the record was compiled. The only exception to this limitation is in a case where the person who originally supplied the information from which the record was compiled is (or would if living be) qualified to give oral expert evidence of that opinion. Quite apart from this, common sense dictates that on such a crucial question of expert evidence, you would not wish to rely on written records, without calling an expert to give oral evidence of his opinion.

Other provisions of the Civil Evidence Act 1968

Sections 2 and 4 of the Act are undoubtedly the most important provisions for all practical purposes. However, it should be noted in passing that by virtue of s. 5(1), certain records produced by computers may be admissible despite their 'hearsay' nature, subject to a variety of safeguards relating to ensuring an accurate supply of information into the computer, and its proper operation.

Section 7 provides for the admissibility of evidence tending to discredit evidence given under ss. 2 or 4, where the maker of a hearsay statement is not called to give evidence.

Giving and receiving notice of proposed hearsay evidence

Sections 2 and 4 of the Civil Evidence Act 1968 represent a considerable departure from the common-law rule against hearsay, and give an advantage to a party who is able to put in such evidence inasmuch as the other side is unable to test the accuracy of that evidence by cross-examination. In order to compensate for this to some degree, s. 8 of the Act provided that rules of the court should be made, regulating the exercise of the right to introduce admissible hearsay evidence. The rules which have been made provide that notice be given of an intention to introduce admissible hearsay evidence under the Act. These rules are set out in full in the appendix to this book, and repay detailed study. In High Court proceedings, they are contained in RSC, Ord. 38, rr. 20–30, and in county court proceedings in CCR, Ord. 20, rr. 15–25.

CCR, Ord. 20, r. 15(1), provides that any party who desires to give in evidence at a trial or hearing any statement which is admissible in evidence by virtue of ss. 2 or 4 shall, not less than 14 days before the day fixed for the trial or hearing, give notice of his desire to do so to the registrar and to every other party. However, this requirement does not apply (unless the court otherwise directs) to an action in which no defence or answer has been filed. This is an important exception, since many proceedings in the county court do go undefended, and it is often overlooked by practitioners. However, even if a defence has not been filed it is sensible if you are relying on hearsay evidence to serve notice: you have then protected your position if a defence is filed late.

The county court has no separate rules governing the content of such notices. Instead, it has been content to adopt the High Court rules dealing with that subject, contained in RSC, Ord. 38, rr. 22–5.

In the case of a statement admissible under s. 2, RSC, Ord. 38, r. 22, provides:

(1) If the statement is admissible by virtue of section 2 of the Act and was made otherwise than in a document, the notice must contain particulars of—

(a) the time, place and circumstances at or in which the statement was made;
(b) the person by whom, and the person to whom, the statement was made; and
(c) the substance of the statement or, if material, the words used.

(2) If the statement is admissible by virtue of the said section 2 and was made in a document, a copy or transcript of the document, or of the relevant part thereof, must be annexed to the notice and the notice must contain such (if any) of the particulars mentioned in paragraph (1)(a) and (b) as are not apparent on the face of the document or part.

This rule would oblige you to state where, when and in what circumstances the Japanese tourist made a statement to Police Constable A, and to set out the gist of what the Japanese tourist said. In the case of the American businessman, you would have to annex to your notice a copy of his statement.

In the case of statements admissible under s. 4, RSC, Ord. 38, r. 23 provides:

(1) If the statement is admissible by virtue of section 4 of the Act, the notice must have annexed to it a copy or transcript of the document containing the statement, or of the relevant part thereof, and must contain—

(a)   particulars of—

(i)   the person by whom the record containing the statement was compiled;

(ii)   any other person through whom that information was supplied to the compiler of that record;

and, in the case of any such person as is referred to in (i) or (ii) above, a description of the duty under which that person was acting when compiling that record or supplying information from which that record was compiled, as the case may be;

(b)   if not apparent on the face of the document annexed to the notice, a description of the nature of the record which, or part of which, contains the statement; and

(c)   particulars of the time, place and circumstances at or in which that record or part was compiled.

As well as containing details of the circumstances in which the hearsay statement is made, the Civil Evidence Act notice must specifically state if it is alleged that the maker *cannot* be called:

If the party giving the notice alleges that any person, particulars of whom are contained in the notice, cannot or should not be called as a witness at the trial or hearing for any of the reasons specified in rule 25, the notice must contain a statement to that effect specifying the reason relied on.

The reasons why a person cannot or should not be called as a witness at the trial are contained both in RSC, Ord. 38, r. 25 and CCR, Ord. 20, r. 17(5). The reason relied upon in any particular notice may be any one or more of the following:

(a)   That the person in question is dead.

(b)   That he is beyond the seas.

(c)   That he is unfit by reason of his bodily or mental condition to attend as a witness.

(d)   That despite the exercise of reasonable diligence it has not been possible to identify or find him.

(e)   That he cannot reasonably be expected to have any recollection of the matters relevant to the accuracy or otherwise of the statement to which the notice relates.

In the example, you will be able to rely on the fact that the American businessman is beyond the seas; you may be able to rely upon some other fact, for example that he is now dead, that you have been unable to find him despite the exercise of reasonable diligence, because he no longer resides in Dallas, or that because of the lapse of time he cannot reasonably be expected to have any recollection of the facts related in his statement. If one or more of these reasons is available, it is essential to include them in the notice. The importance of this cannot be overstated, and is as follows.

Change sides for a moment, and suppose that you represent the defendant in the civil action arising from the accident. In good time before trial, you are served with a Civil Evidence Act notice stating that the American businessman is beyond the seas and therefore cannot be called as a witness, and that the plaintiff intends to put into evidence his hearsay statement. You are now faced with the difficulty that potentially damaging evidence will be presented to the court without being subjected to cross-examination. What can be done?

In some cases, there is a remedy. CCR, Ord. 20, r. 17(1), provides that any party on whom a Civil Evidence Act notice is served may, within seven days after service of the notice, give to the registrar and the party who served the notice a counter-notice requiring that the person named in the Civil Evidence Act notice, should be called as a witness at the trial. This means the party serving the counter-notice can insist that the witness is available for cross-examination, instead of merely accepting his hearsay statement. The important point, however, is that the counter-notice procedure is not available in all cases. Order 20, r. 17(2) provides:

Where any notice under rule 15 contains a statement that any person particulars of whom are contained in the notice cannot or should not be called as a witness for the reason specified therein, a party shall not be entitled to serve a counter-notice under this rule requiring that person to be called as a witness at the trial or hearing unless he contends that that person can or, as the case may be, should be called, and in that case he must include in his counter-notice a statement to that effect.

From this, it is clear that the counter-notice is a far less effective weapon where the Civil Evidence Act notice has contained a statement that the witness cannot or should not be called for one of the reasons set out in r. 17(5). In such a case the effect of the counter-notice is to force your opponent to prove that his assertion that the witness cannot be called (or has no recollection) is in fact true. Where the original notice contains a statement that a witness cannot or should not be called, and a counter-notice is served disputing that fact, the proper course is to apply to the court for a determination of that question before trial. Provision for this is made by Ord. 20, r. 18.

In almost every case, the server of the counter-notice has a very difficult task. Any one of the reasons set forth in r. 17(5) is sufficient to enable the server of the Civil Evidence Act notice to put in the hearsay statement without calling the witness. For example, if your Japanese witness is beyond the seas, that is in itself a sufficient reason why he cannot or should not be called. It is then unnecessary to show that reasonable diligence has been exercised to find out precisely where he is or to make him available as a witness [3].

The inclusion of such reasons in a Civil Evidence Act notice therefore has very dramatic effects. Provided you can demonstrate that one of the reasons specified in r. 17(5) applies, the statement is admissible at trial, and any counter-notice is wholly ineffective. In such a case, your opponent has no remedy except to comment as forcefully as possible upon the weight of the hearsay evidence, in the light of the fact that he has been unable to test it by cross-examination.

Because all advocates are from time to time subject to inadvertence, you should be aware of the provisions of CCR, Ord. 20, r. 20. This allows the court, where it thinks it just to do so, to exercise its discretion in favour of allowing a hearsay statement to be admitted under ss. 2 or 4 of the 1968 Act, even though the party has failed to serve a Civil Evidence Act notice. The court may be prepared in exceptional cases to allow an adjournment to enable a notice to be served, though in such a case the party at fault may clearly be required to pay the costs thrown away. The court will not, however, exercise its discretion in such a party's favour where there has been a deliberate disregard of the rules rather than mere inadvertence [4].

Illustration of Civil Evidence Act notice

Take notice that at the trial of this action the plaintiff desires to give on evidence the statement made on the following document namely, a letter dated 26 September 1983 from Mr John Smith to the plaintiff's solicitors.

A copy of the said document is annexed hereto. And further take notice that Mr John Smith cannot be called as a witness at the trial because he is in Melbourne, Victoria, Australia.

Notes

1. *H* v *Schering Chemicals Ltd* [1983] 1 WLR 143.
2. *Savings & Investment Bank Ltd* v *Gasco Investments (Netherlands) BV* [1984] 1 WLR 271.
3. *Rasool* v *West Midlands Passenger Transport Executive* [1974] 3 All ER 638; *Piermay Shipping Co. SA* v *Chester* [1978] 1 WLR 411.
4. Compare *Ford* v *Lewis* [1971] 1 WLR 623 with *Morris* v *Stratford-on-Avon RDC* [1973] 1 WLR 1059.

Four

Confessions and the Judges' Rules

Introduction

It is the moment that every defence advocate dreads. It is the moment when the advocate hears the officer say, 'In reply to the caution, the defendant said . . .' or: 'The defendant then elected to make a written statement under caution which I now produce'. And you know what is coming next. The more matter-of-fact the officer's voice, the worse it is probably going to be. All advocates who practise in the criminal courts have experienced their own personal nightmare, and secretly fear the defence advocates' race-memory of some occasion on which some mythical defendant admitted everything and added his theft of the Crown Jewels to boot. It runs something like this: 'All right, guv', it's a fair cop. You got me bang to rights. I suppose with form like mine it will be straight inside this time.'

This is a therapeutic chapter, written for those haunted by the unspoken but deeply felt fear of the denouement described above. We may as well start by facing facts. There is nothing that any advocate can do about a confession freely and voluntarily made, in full compliance with the Judges' Rules. A properly taken confession is admissible and powerful evidence of guilt, and rightly so. No prosecuting advocate should ever feel embarrassed about inviting a bench to convict on the evidence of a confession, even in the absence of other evidence, provided that the confession was made freely and voluntarily.

Let us start by considering what a confession is. A confession is the name given to an adverse admission made by the defendant in a criminal case which suggests or confirms his guilt of the offence charged. In common parlance, the word 'confession' implies a full admission of guilt, even a hint of melodrama. But the word carries no such implication in law. Any admission which, even partially, tends to incriminate the maker in the offence charged is termed a confession. A confession may be made orally, in the course of an interview between the defendant and the police officer, or in writing in the form of a statement under caution. In cases involving serious charges, it is now a common practice for the content of an interview to be reduced to writing by a 'scribe', so that a written record exists of the question-and-answer session, even where the confession has been made verbally.

Those who have made a careful study of Chapter 2 will ask why such an admission should be admissible, since it appears to fall squarely within the definition of hearsay which we there considered. That is an intelligent and proper question. The answer to it is that at common law, admissions adverse to the interests of the maker are admissible, in both civil and criminal cases [1], as evidence of the facts admitted, as an exception to the rule against hearsay. The justification for this exception is that a voluntary admission by a party, contrary to that party's interest, is inherently reliable because of the unlikelihood of its being made except from a desire to tell the truth. Admissions against interest have always been regarded as evidence not only admissible, but also extremely cogent against the party making the admission.

The above observations are valid only where the admission (or confession, as we shall call it in this chapter, following the terminology in criminal cases) is made freely and voluntarily and in compliance with the Judges' Rules. In a surprising number of instances, defence advocates are unaware of legitimate arguments which might be made to exclude or limit evidence of confessions, and prosecutors are unaware of potential weaknesses or potential strengths in their cases based on confessions. We hope that some of these problems will be resolved by what follows in this chapter.

Taking instructions about confessions

As a matter of practical preparation, there are few areas as crucial as confessions, so far as the taking of detailed instructions is concerned. Cross-examination of police officers is almost impossible without a vivid and detailed understanding of the circumstances in which an interview occurred, or a written statement under caution was made. In what place; at what time of day or night; in what frame of mind; whether it was the defendant's first experience of a police station;

whether the defendant was allowed access to a solicitor. With each day that passes before instructions are taken, the defendant's memory will tend to fade, and perhaps even be subconsciously repressed, whereas the police officer's recollection is permanently recorded in his notes or in the recesses of his professional experience. If the period of detention and interrogation was long, the problem is intensified. Yet, in order to have a serious chance of success in cross-examination about a confession, it is vital to have a full account of what happened: how many interviews; in what order; who was present; and most importantly, what did the officer say and what did your client say? Unless you can challenge or otherwise deal with the detail of the confession line by line, your cross-examination will lose something in terms of effectiveness. Similarly with a written statement under caution. How long did it take to make? Who wrote what? Did they record word for word what your client said? Were any questions interposed as he was dictating? Did he sign the statement and initial any corrections? Was he told that he could correct, alter or add anything he wished?

Obviously, an early and lengthy conference with your client is called for if you are to have any hope of getting instructions of this kind. In many cases, for good reason or bad, the defendant will be unable to give you instructions in sufficient detail. If this happens, you must do what you can with the available material. But this should not be accepted as an inevitable problem, and must not be permitted to occur simply because of your failure to take the best possible instructions.

When dealing with a written statement under caution, you should always insist on seeing the original, preferably before trial. Things leap out of the pages of an original which may be buried in a typed or even a photographic copy. Nuances of signature (steady or shaky?) of handwriting (hurried or leisurely?) or corrections (fluent or hesitant?) become devastatingly apparent in many cases. The original should also give away many secrets about the time a statement must have taken to write, about the frame of mind of the maker and the willingness or otherwise of the maker to make the statement. From both the original and the copy, you may gain a useful insight from the language used. Is this the style of language your client habitually employs? Are there words or phrases which he could not spell or even understand? In dealing with clients to whom English is a second language, this can be a particularly fertile field of inquiry.

Admissibility of confessions

Confessions are admissible at common law in criminal cases, as an exception to the rule against hearsay. The rationale for this exception is to be found in the assumption which the law is prepared to make, that a confession may be regarded as reliable because such an adverse admission, contrary to the interests of the maker, is unlikely to have been made unless true. The suspicion of unreliability traditionally associated with most hearsay evidence is therefore perceived to be outweighed by the presumptive reliability of a confession. Of course, this proposition holds good only where the confession is shown to have been made freely and voluntarily. If it is extorted by threats or inducements, or is the product of fear or hope of advantage rather than the willingness to confess, its reliability is obviously compromised. A confession which is not free and voluntary is a grave threat to a fair trial, since there is no objection to the court convicting on evidence of a confession alone, in the absence of other evidence, if it is persuaded that it would be right to do so.

For the above reasons it is a well established rule of English criminal law that a confession made to a person in authority will be admitted as evidence of the guilt of the maker only if the prosecution prove beyond reasonable doubt that the confession was made voluntarily and in the absence of oppression. This rule should be engraved on the memory of every criminal advocate, for the frequency with which confessions are tendered to the court, and the peculiar evidential weight which a confession may enjoy, make it one of the most important of all rules of evidence. This is underlined by the fact that the prosecution must prove the admissibility of a confession (assuming that this is disputed) to the same standard of proof as is required for the proof of guilt itself, despite the fact that the standard required for demonstrating the admissibility of evidence in other respects is the balance of probabilities.

Persons in authority   The rule applies only to confessions made to a 'person in authority'. This is no real weakening of the rule, since virtually all confessions are made to persons in authority. A person in authority is anyone who is involved in the arrest, detention or prosecution of the defendant, and who consequently has, or may reasonably be thought by the defendant to have some influence or control over the case against him. In other words, these are persons from whom some threat of prejudice or hope of advantage may appear to the defendant to be credible, and who are therefore the persons most likely, whether or not intentionally, to provoke a confession which is not free and voluntary. Persons in authority are dealing with the defendant from a position of power, and not on equal terms. Sometimes, a defendant makes a spontaneous confession to a friend or relative or someone else who is not a person in authority, and in this comparatively rare case, it is held that the receiver of the confession has no such influence over the defendant, but deals with the defendant on equal terms. In such cases, the confession is admissible as a matter of law regardless of the circumstances in which it is obtained, although, as in the case of any other confession, the court may exclude as a matter of discretion and in the interests of securing a fair trial.

There is no closed category of persons in authority. Police officers are by far the most common example, but case-law and common sense also include, among others, Customs and Excise officers, investigators employed by the Inland Revenue and the Department of Health and Social Security, store detectives and, in relation to military personnel, officers of superior rank. Quite apart from professional investigators, the loser of stolen goods or the victim, complainant or prosecutor may be persons in authority because of their interest in the outcome of the prosecution. Occasionally, it is unclear whether a person is a person in authority, and the court may have to decide this as a question of fact: for example, the mere fact that a person is a prosecution witness is not enough to make that person a person in authority [2], in the absence of the necessary relationship to the arrest, detention or prosecution of the defendant. The court may have to look closely at the facts of the case, in order to make this determination. One odd instance worth remembering is that a police surgeon, called to examine a defendant, is not regarded as a person in authority, because he is regarded as an independent expert witness: *R* v *Nowell* [3]. Although this rule is, to say the least, unrealistic (and has been rejected in Scotland) it must be remembered specifically, as it is not infrequently important.

In *R* v *Cleary* [4] the defendant made a confession in response to an inducement made by his father, in the presence of two senior police officers, who did not dissent from what the father said. Although the father was not a person in authority, the officers were, and it was held that the situation presented by their presence and failure to dissent was equivalent to a case where the confession was made directly to a person in authority. Consequently, the confession, which was plainly not voluntary, should have been excluded.

Voluntariness The classic pronouncement on the subject of voluntariness was made by Lord Sumner in his speech in *Ibrahim* v *R* [5]. Its forcefulness has not diminished over the years, and it is still very well worth citing in argument:

> It has long been established as a positive rule of English criminal law, that no statement by an accused is admissible in evidence against him unless it is shown by the prosecution to have been a voluntary statement, in the sense that it has not been obtained from him either by fear of prejudice or hope of advantage exercised [6] or held out by a person in authority.

It will be clear from this passage that 'voluntary', in the context of confessions, has a specialised meaning. It is not used in its popular sense, and is not concerned with the question of whether the defendant was eager or reluctant to confess, or whether he exhibited bravado or remorse in his attitude. What is meant by a confession being voluntary or involuntary is that the confession was or was not induced by some threat or inducement which had the effect of eliminating or undermining the defendant's freedom to choose whether or not to make a confession, or what confession to make.

Whether a confession has been obtained by fear of prejudice or hope of advantage is a question of fact in each case. The categories of fears and hopes are not closed. But even if not closed, the categories become familiar to every practising advocate through sheer repetition. Allegations of fear of prejudice and hope of advantage are made and refuted daily in criminal courts throughout the country, and seem to change rather little over the course of time. A confession in return for abstention from violence, in return for bail, in return for forbearing to bring other charges, in return for allowing other offences to be taken into consideration, in return for a mitigating word to the bench, in return for not arresting or charging some other member of the family.

Although it has been said judicially that the court will be 'at pains to hold that even the most gentle . . . threats or slight inducements will taint a confession' [7], and although the prosecution bear the burden of proving beyond reasonable doubt that a confession is admissible, in any case where its admissibility is disputed by the defence, every defence advocate knows that it is formidably difficult to have a confession excluded in a magistrates' court. One reason for this may be the natural, but mistaken tendency of a bench to feel that the exclusion of a confession necessarily implies some criticism of the police officers involved in obtaining the confession. There can be no doubt that in many cases, such feelings inhibit the making of rulings adverse to the prosecution. Often, of course, the exclusion of a confession obtained by police officers does, in reality, involve some such implication by virtue of the very gravity of the allegations made by the defendant. But equally often, you may be able to point out to the bench that the ruling for which you are asking does not require them to commit themselves to any censure of the officers.

There are two excellent arguments which you should present in this respect. The first is that, since the prosecution have the burden of proof on the issue of admissibility, it is fatal to the confession if the bench have any reasonable doubt, or feel less than sure about the admissibility of the confession. They need not make any positive finding with regard to the defendant's allegations, much less any positive finding that the officers have acted culpably. The second is that it does not matter whether the circumstances which led to a confession being made involuntarily were created deliberately or by accident. In other words, it is the state of mind of the defendant, not that of the officers which counts, and the defence need not suggest any intention to offer any fear or inducement [8]. The bench may quite properly find that a confession is inadmissible because some fear or inducement was suggested unintentionally and even with the best of motives. In the case of an inexperienced defendant who finds himself in a police station, being interrogated about an offence, for the first time in his life, this is by no means an uncommon situation. The defendant may well believe that the police were deliberately threatening or deceptive, but the evidence may show a more innocent situation, which makes the case for exclusion far more palatable to the court. Similar arguments are available where the case for exclusion is that the defendant's capacity to make a voluntary confession was reduced or eliminated by the effects of alcohol or drugs [9], or by misleading information [10] or where the desire for release was exacerbated by ill-health, pain or even extreme nervousness.

The issue of voluntariness is, therefore, a matter not only of whether some threat or inducement was made, but also of whether such a threat or inducement was actually a factor in the making of the confession. There is no such thing as a threat or inducement which is enough to exclude a confession as a matter of law; it is a question of fact whether the confession was voluntary, in every case. Although there are cases, for example where a confession is extorted by violence, where it is inconceivable that a court would hold the resulting confession to be voluntary, the issue is still one of fact. The vast majority of cases are far less clear-cut, and involve an examination of the character and circumstances of the defendant, his experience or inexperience with police procedure, his record, if any, the gravity of the offence and the seriousness of the alleged threat or inducement. Hence the need for careful and thorough instructions in all such cases.

The case for exclusion is always a difficult one to argue, since the bench will, quite naturally and rightly, tend to want to hear all the available evidence, and to resent attempts to keep evidence out. To persuade them that fairness to the defence requires exclusion is never an easy task. The best prospects for success are afforded by emphasis on the burden and standard of proof, and by the minimisation of any suggestion of deliberate misconduct on the part of the officers. The latter technique is, of course, available only where consistent with the evidence; it is pointless and self-defeating to sacrifice all sense of reality by arguing for an unintentional inducement in a case where, if the defendant is to be believed, the officers were plainly guilty of gross misconduct. In such a case, it is essential to argue the misconduct forcefully and fearlessly. Only professional judgment will supply the most cogent line of argument in an individual case, but the two techniques offered above have a proven record of success, which must have something to do with the fact that they offer a way to exclude without the need to invade the forbidden territory of police misconduct. The following words of Lord Reid in *Commissioners of Customs & Excise* v *Harz* [11] are comforting and well worth citing in argument:

> It is true that many of the so-called inducements have been so vague that no reasonable man would have been influenced by them, but one must remember that not all accused are reasonable men or women: they may be very ignorant and terrified by the

predicament in which they find themselves. So it may have been right to err on the safe side.

Absence of oppression   It is doubtful whether the requirement that the confession should have been obtained without oppression adds anything to the requirement of voluntariness. It is even something of a mystery how the requirement came into being. It is generally ascribed to Lord Parker CJ who, in *Callis* v *Gunn* [12], said:

> There is a fundamental principle of law that no answer to a question and no statement is admissible unless it is shown by the prosecution *not to have been obtained in an oppressive manner* and to have been voluntary in the sense that it has not been obtained by threats or inducements. (Emphasis added.)

When the Judges' Rules appeared in revised form in 1964, both the voluntary nature of the confession and its freedom from oppression were stated to be parts of a principle of law which was to be 'overriding and applicable in all cases'. Since then, the absence of oppression has been treated as a requirement of admissibility, though its main usefulness, when perceived as an accumulation to the requirement of voluntariness, probably lies in the additional emphasis which argument to the court gains from the inclusion of a second definition of much the same thing. Sachs J in *R* v *Priestly* [13], offered a description of oppression which sounds, and was no doubt intended to sound, very much like a description of circumstances from which it would be reasonable to infer that a confession was not voluntary. He referred to such matters as the length of periods of questioning and the characteristics of the person making the confession. The learned judge added: 'What may be oppressive as regards a child, an invalid or an old man or somebody inexperienced in the ways of this world may turn out not to be oppressive when one finds that the accused person is of a tough character and an experienced man of the world.'

Discretionary exclusion of confessions: the Judges' Rules

The Judges' Rules are rules laid down by the judges of the Queen's Bench Division of the High Court for the guidance of police officers and other professional investigators involved in the conduct of interrogations, and in the arrest or detention of suspected or accused persons. They were first promulgated in 1912 by the judges of the then King's Bench Division, and have since been revised. If the Police and Criminal Evidence Bill or some future version thereof becomes law, there will be substantial changes in the area of the law dealing with the treatment of persons in custody, and these changes will inevitably affect the rules of evidence concerning confessions. Unfortunately, it cannot be said with any degree of certainty at the time of writing what the outcome of the Bill's controversial passage through Parliament will be. For the time being, a working knowledge of the present Judges' Rules is essential for every practitioner in the criminal courts, and that knowledge should be sufficient to permit the advocate to refer to them without hesitation during a trial, and to be able to demonstrate to the bench any apparent breach.

One reason why a knowledge of the rules is so important should be obvious in the light of the foregoing discussion of the principles of admissibility of confessions. Although due observance of the Judges' Rules is not a guarantee that a confession was made voluntarily and without oppression, compliance or non-compliance with the rules is good evidence one way or the other, and makes very cogent material for argument on the issue of admissibility.

Quite apart from the usefulness of the rules on the issue of admissibility, for the purposes of making some judgment of the circumstances in which a confession was taken, the Judges' Rules have a further value to the defence advocate. If the defence can show a breach of the Judges' Rules, concerned with the arrest or detention of the defendant or the obtaining of a confession, the court may, as a matter not of law but of discretion, exclude the confession in the interests of fairness to the defendant [14]. It is important to note that a breach of the rules does not render the confession inadmissible as a matter of law, unless the court concludes that the breach may have resulted in oppressive circumstances, or in the confession being made involuntarily. The breach merely presents the court with one reason to exercise the exclusionary discretion, which was examined in Chapter 1, in the interests of securing a fair trial for the defendant.

Therefore, a breach of the Judges' Rules provides the defence advocate with two arguments in favour of excluding the confession. Both should be advanced, and the court should be referred specifically to the rule or rules which have been breached. A bench which is vacillating over the admissibility of a confession can sometimes be persuaded by evidence of an undeniable breach of the rules simply because the court is presented with a readily identifiable ground for its ruling. You should not, of course, neglect the fact that it is the securing of a fair trial for the defendant that matters. Unless you persuade the court that some unfairness may well result from the breach of the rules, the discretion will not be exercised in your client's favour. A breach, in and of itself, is insufficient reason to exclude. To evaluate the significance of a breach requires professional judgment. A trivial breach, which may evoke some expression of disapproval from the court, but which clearly had little or no effect on the defendant or his rights, should be played down or mentioned in passing, rather than beaten to death in argument.

Recognising breaches of the Judges' Rules

Even given a thorough working knowledge of the Judges' Rules, it is obvious that the range of possible breaches is not inconsiderable, and that a breach may not always be easy to recognise. In summary trial, working without copies of the prosecution statements, this can present problems for the defence advocate in identifying areas of complaint while there is still time to act on them. One useful technique in overcoming this problem is to carry a check-list of areas in which a breach is most likely to emerge. Your client's instructions will assist in alerting you to the most probable areas in any particular case. The areas which require most attention are those involving: (a) the arrest or detention of the defendant; (b) the defendant's right of access to a solicitor while in custody; (c) the use of appropriate cautions; and (d) the method of taking written statements under caution.

Arrest and detention The introductory preamble to the Judges' Rules explains that the rules do not affect certain fundamental principles of law, among which are the principles:

(b) That police officers, otherwise than by arrest, cannot compel any person against his will to come to or remain in any police station; . . .

(d) That when a police officer who is making inquiries of any person about an offence has enough evidence to prefer a charge against that person for the offence, he should without delay cause that person to be charged or informed that he may be prosecuted for the offence.

A valid arrest requires that the officer make it clear to the person arrested, if it is not clear from the circumstances, that he is under arrest and for what alleged offence he is under arrest. The following words of Lawton LJ in *R* v *Lemsatef* [15] sufficiently indicate the importance with which the law regards these principles:

> Neither arrest nor detention can properly be carried out without the accused person being told the offence for which he is being arrested. There is no such offence as 'helping police with their inquiries'. This is a phrase which has crept into use, largely because of the need for the press to be careful about how they report what has happened when somebody has been arrested but not charged. If the idea is getting around amongst . . . police officers that they can arrest or detain people, as the case may be, for this particular purpose, the sooner they disabuse themselves of that idea, the better.

A confession obtained following an unlawful arrest or during unlawful detention is subject to strong objection. A continued detention in breach of principle (d) which results in a confession is also assailable in terms of rule 3(b), which designates the stage at which a suspect should be charged or informed that he may be prosecuted for the offence, as the stage at which interrogation should be discontinued. The rule provides that:

> It is only in exceptional cases that questions relating to the offence should be put to the accused person after he has been charged or informed that he may be prosecuted. Such questions may be put where they are necessary for the purpose of preventing or minimising harm or loss to some other person or to the public or for clearing up an ambiguity in a previous answer or statement.

Rule 3(b) goes on to provide a specific form of caution for use before such exceptional questioning, and to require the making of a contemporaneous written record thereof. The purpose of these rules is to ensure that interrogation is limited to its proper purpose of the investigation of a suspected offence. When an officer has 'enough evidence' to charge or inform the defendant that he may be prosecuted is something of a movable feast, and the officer is allowed considerable leeway to use his judgment. But occasionally, this judgment can be attacked effectively in cross-examination with a view to showing that a confession was obtained during interrogation conducted in breach of rule 3(b).

The word 'charged' in rule 3 and principle (d) means formally charged with the offence, not merely accused of it during interrogation [16], and the phrase 'informed that he may be prosecuted' refers to a case where the suspect has not been arrested, but the police contemplate the issue of a summons [17].

Access to a solicitor   Another fundamental principle unaffected by the Judges' Rules is:

>   (c)   That every person at any stage of an investigation should be able to communicate and consult privately with a solicitor. This is so even if he is in custody provided that in such a case no unreasonable delay or hindrance is caused to the processes of investigation or the administration of justice by his doing so.

This is a most sensitive issue. No police officer is going to say in the witness-box that he did not wish a suspect to see his solicitor because he feared that the suspect might be advised to remain silent. It is not uncommon, on the other hand, for an officer to say that he prevented or delayed a meeting between the suspect and his solicitor because of some apprehended hindrance to the processes of investigation or the administration of justice. Skilful cross-examination can often cast doubt on the purity of this motive, since except in limited circumstances, it sounds at best unconvincing to ascribe consequences adverse to the processes of investigation or the administration of justice to the presence of an officer of the Supreme Court. Note this useful, ringing phrase to include in your cross-examination. It sounds much more forceful than the single word 'solicitor'. The limited circumstances arise where there is a substantial prospect of messages being passed via the defendant's friends or relatives, which might assist suspects still at large or result in the destruction of evidence.

It is clear law that it is improper for an officer to refuse a suspect access to a solicitor because the suspect has not made a confession, or because he might be advised to remain silent, and a confession made after denial of access to a solicitor should be strenuously challenged: *R* v *Lemsatef* [18]. In taking instructions, do not forget to ask your client whether he made an appropriate request to see a solicitor: the police are not obliged to press your services upon a suspect [19].

Use of appropriate cautions   The requirements of the Judges' Rules that a suspect should be cautioned at certain stages of an inquiry are very important. The caution does not create a right to silence, but reminds the suspect of a right which he already possesses in law: *Hall* v *R* [20]. There are two cautions of general importance, and the evidence should be scrutinised with care to see whether and when they were administered. These are known respectively as the rule 2 and rule 3 cautions.

Rule 2 provides:

> As soon as a police officer has evidence which would afford reasonable grounds for suspecting that a person has committed an offence, he shall caution that person or cause him to be cautioned before putting to him any questions, or further questions, relating to that offence.
>
> The caution shall be in the following terms: 'You are not obliged to say anything unless you wish to do so but what you say may be put into writing and given in evidence.'

The use of the mandatory word 'shall' indicates that a confession obtained without caution, at or after the stage where the officer has evidence affording reasonable grounds for suspecting that the defendant has committed an offence, has been obtained in breach of the rules. But once again, the officer must be given considerable leeway in determining when that stage has arrived, unless it is clear from the facts facing the officer, for example where he has apparently caught a suspect red-handed. It has been held that the evidence referred to must be admissible evidence, which the officer could put before a court as the beginnings of a case, and not mere suspicion [21]. The officer can therefore go some way with his investigation before his duty to caution under rule 2 arises, and it is accordingly difficult to demonstrate a breach of the rule. However, there are cases where the rule 2 caution is improperly omitted, and where this is exposed in cross-examination, it creates a strong argument in favour of excluding a resulting confession.

Rule 3(a) provides:

> Where a person is charged with or informed that he may be prosecuted for an offence he shall be cautioned in the following terms: 'Do you wish to say anything? You are not obliged to say anything unless you wish to do so but whatever you say will be taken down in writing and may be given in evidence.'

It is rare for this caution to be omitted, and its timing is very specific. Moreover, confessions have usually been made by the stage of the rule 3 caution. There is an importance in the rule, however, because this stage also operates as the cut-off point for interrogation about the offence in question. Except in the unusual circumstances set forth in rule 3(b) (see above under 'Arrest and detention'), any response to the rule 3 caution should therefore be the defendant's last word.

Taking of statements under caution Rule 4 lays down in considerable detail the proper manner of taking written statements under caution. The formal declarations required by rule 4 are usually correctly inserted into the statement, though it is often questionable whether the defendant read or understood them. Most of the problems in this area arise from allegations that the substantive portion of the statement is not in the defendant's words, but those of the officer, or that the defendant was compelled to sign the statement, or to sign without reading it through.

The rule actually protects the officer as much as the defendant. The suspect is asked to sign two declarations, contained in rule 4(a), (c) and (e) acknowledging the truth and voluntariness of the statement, that it is made of the suspect's own free will and that he has been given the opportunity to add, alter or correct anything he wishes. Where the defendant has signed these declarations, they make excellent material for cross-examination, if the defendant gives evidence. Even though the defendant may allege that he did not sign freely, there is something about repeated signatures of specifically worded declarations which affords a skilful prosecutor valuable ammunition for exposing false allegations of oppression or involuntariness.

Although the above check-list is not exhaustive, it does draw attention to the most common situations in which a breach of the

Judges' Rules may be revealed. It should be noted that, by rule 6, professional investigators other than police officers, for example store detectives, are enjoined to comply with the rules, 'so far as practicable'.

Challenging the weight of confessions

If the bench find that a confession is admissible in law, as being voluntary and made in the absence of oppression, and further find that there is no ground to exclude the confession in the exercise of their discretion, the confession will be admitted in evidence. Some defence advocates seem to give up at this point, and assume that there is nothing more that they can do. This is far from the truth. The bench have ruled only on admissibility, and the whole question of weight remains open to challenge. This may be done during cross-examination of the officers, and by calling your client and other witnesses, and of course during your closing speech. It is important, of course, to bear in mind that the issue is no longer just voluntariness or the absence of oppression, but whether the bench should give the confession enough weight to justify their acting on it to convict.

Confessions implicating co-defendants

It is a cardinal rule of evidence that any adverse admission, including a confession, is evidence against the maker of the admission only, and not against any other person implicated by it [22]. Because the maker may have had motives of his own for implicating others, and because the person or persons implicated had no opportunity to be present and refute what was said about them by the maker, the implication against those others is inherently unreliable, and would not justify the departure from the rule against hearsay that would be necessary to render the admission admissible against them.

It is, of course, commonplace for one defendant to try to put the blame on another, or at least to try to share the blame with another, and a confession, particularly a written statement under caution, is an ideal tool for the job. This poses an intractable procedural and evidential problem if the defendants are tried jointly. Suppose that you represent defendant A. Defendant B, jointly charged and tried with A, has made a written statement under caution implicating A. The prosecution wish to place B's confession before the bench, because, even if it is not evidence against A, it is certainly evidence against B as the maker. The very fact that B has tried to implicate A in a certain way may even be cogent evidence against B himself. On the other hand, if the confession goes before the court, there will be prejudice to A, consisting of evidence which is not admissible against A.

In almost every case, the confession will be admitted in full, and the prejudice to A must be accepted as one of the risks of a joint trial. Nor will the situation be an adequate ground for separate trials, unless the prejudice is very great. Although this seems unfair on the face of it, the rule does correspond to certain of the realities of practice. Firstly, the prosecution are entitled to use the confession against B. Secondly, the confession should be admitted as a whole unless there are very good reasons for not doing so, because the court should ordinarily be told exactly what a defendant states in his confession. Thirdly, the evidential value of the confession as against B would be weakened by omitting the reference to A. Fourthly, the confession may effectively be made evidence against A in the course of your cross-examination of B. Although B's out-of-court statement is not evidence against A, what B says from the witness-box on oath at the trial is evidence in the case generally. In many cases, you will be unable to cross-examine effectively without referring to the statement, and there is accordingly no real ground for excluding the passages referring to A, to which B's advocate will be entitled to refer during re-examination, in order to re-establish B's credibility.

In most cases, you will wish to cross-examine B as strenuously as possible, since the best way to nullify the effect of his confession is to demonstrate his dishonesty or unreliability. Remember always that the order of cross-examination dictates that you must cross-examine B before the prosecutor does so. Even if you ask no questions about that part of B's confession which concerns A, the prosecutor will, and you may have no chance to rebut whatever B says in answer to that cross-examination. In short, it is almost always a serious mistake not to cross-examine B fully. You may as well face the full impact of the statement and try to demolish it.

Certainly, there are cases where the reference to A is relatively insignificant to the case against B, and where the risk of prejudice to A is very great, where the court should either grant separate trials or agree to the editing of B's statement [23]. Any application for such relief should, of course, be made by explaining the position to the bench in general terms, without referring to the details of the evidence, so as to avoid exposing the bench to prejudicial material.

It is the duty of A's advocate, in the situation where B's confession is admitted without editing on a joint trial, to remind the bench very forcefully that nothing in the statement is evidence against A. This must be done deliberately and pointedly in the course of your closing speech. Make a point of emphasising that B's statement is not evidence against A for any purpose, and that the prosecution cannot rely on the statement to prove the case against A.

Confessions made in response to confessions of co-defendants

In certain cases, defendant A may make a confession after being shown a written statement under caution made by defendant B, whether or not the written statement actually implicates A. Although B's statement is not evidence against A, for the reasons discussed above, what A says to the police in response to B's statement may be evidence against A if it amounts to a confession. This is sometimes described as A adopting B's statement, though it is actually A's own statement that is evidence against him. The prosecution may, of course, refer to B's statement in such a case, in order to explain or provide the background for A's statement. If, having been shown B's statement, A denies what B says, then he has in no way adopted B's statement, and in this case neither A's denial nor B's statement have any evidential value against A.

Where both A and B have been charged with an offence, or informed that they may be prosecuted for the offence, and a police officer wishes at that stage to show B's statement under caution to A, the Judges' Rules provide restrictions on what may be done, because the cut-off point for interrogation for the offence has passed, and there are obvious dangers in inviting A to comment on B's statement at that stage. Rule 5 provides that in such circumstances, the officer shall:

> hand to that person [A] a true copy of such written statement, but nothing shall be said or done to invite any reply or comment. If that person says that he would like to make a statement in reply, or starts to say something, he shall at once be cautioned or further cautioned as prescribed in rule 3(a).

Whether or not rule 5 applies, you should take very careful instructions about the circumstances in which B's statement was shown to A, particularly where the police officers have recorded that A has agreed with the statement, with some such phrase as 'Well, if B has told you all about it, there's nothing I can say.' Such a situation is very likely to arise, particularly where there has been a breach of rule 5. Your client may not know or understand why B said what he did, but may have assumed that B would be believed, rather than he himself. It is essential to identify the dangers in each individual situation, and deal with them in cross-examination and by adducing evidence, and if possible, excluding any adoption by A of B's statement.

Confessions which reveal previous bad character

It is desirable that a confession should be made in the defendant's own words. This occasionally has disadvantages for the defence, in that the defendant himself may refer in his statement to some matter which is inadmissible against him, but which has the potential for prejudice. A reference to previous bad character is the most usual example. Although the prosecution would not be permitted to use the defendant's bad character as evidence of his guilt, the defendant may not object, as a matter of strict law, to the admission of his statement containing the unfortunate revelation [24].

In practice, however, a more lenient rule generally prevails, since references to character are incidental and accidental, and add nothing to the evidential value of the confession. The practice is to edit out of the statement the offending references. This is achieved, in the case of a written confession, by physically striking the passages concerned (providing edited copies for the use of the court) and in the case of an oral statement, by instructing the witnesses to omit the passages from their evidence (to avoid accidental allusions, it is advisable to have the officers mark their notebooks in pencil, and have the prosecutor use leading questions to avoid the offending passages and maintain a smooth narrative). The practice of editing in these circumstances enjoys the express sanction of the courts [25], and responsible prosecutors will unhesitatingly agree to defence requests for such editing, unless the case is an unusual one. Unusual cases, in which editing may not be appropriate, are those where the confession would be so emasculated by the editing as to be wholly or virtually unintelligible to the bench (in which case the confession should either be omitted altogether, or presented to the bench intact with copious warnings to ignore the reference to character), or cases where the reference to character actually has some relevance to guilt, for example where the defendant's admission of his presence in prison at a given time proves his association with a co-defendant (in which case the prosecution can and should insist upon the statement going into evidence as it stands).

In any case where the statement is presented to the bench without editing, it is the duty of the defence advocate to emphasise to the bench that the reference to bad character has no evidential value in proving the defendant's guilt. But it should be stressed that such a situation ought to be exceptional.

Admissibility of the defendant's silence and self-serving statements

Not every defendant confesses. Some remain stoically silent, while others vigorously assert their innocence. An understanding of how and why these situations differ from those presented by confessions is important in many cases.

The defendant's silence in the face of accusations of an offence cannot, at common law, be held to be evidence of his guilt on the basis that his failure to rebut the charges amounts to an adverse admission. Hence the observation made earlier in this chapter that the caution does not create a right to silence, but merely reminds the suspect of a right which he already enjoys. In *Hall* v *R* [26], Lord Diplock said:

It is a clear and widely known principle of the common law . . . that a person is entitled to refrain from answering a question put to him for the purpose of discovering whether he has committed a criminal offence. *A fortiori* he is under no obligation to comment when he is informed that someone else has accused him of an offence. It may be that in very exceptional circumstances an inference may be drawn from a failure to give an explanation or a disclaimer, but in their Lordships' view, silence alone, on being informed by a police officer that someone else has made an accusation against him, cannot give rise to an inference that the person to whom this information is communicated accepts the truth of the accusation.

The reference to 'very exceptional circumstances' in Lord Diplock's speech relates back to a dictum of Cave J in *R* v *Mitchell* [27], in which that learned judge held that some inference of guilt might be drawn where the suspect and his accuser were speaking 'on even terms'.

It is not clear what is meant by speaking 'on even terms'. Two potential situations have been identified. The first is where the suspect is confronted by an accuser who is not a person in authority, for example a relative of the victim of the offence [28]. The second arises where the defendant is being interrogated in the presence of his solicitor, who is allowed to advise the defendant about his answers [29]. Neither situation would necessarily give rise to even terms in every case, and conversely, other situations may be identified where even terms would result. The key may be whether the defendant is in any sense subject to the authority of the questioner; unless the answer to this question is an unqualified negative, the courts will be slow to erode the traditional common-law rule that there is a right to silence without adverse inference being drawn from that silence. Certainly, in the normal police interrogation, the defendant is not on even terms with the officer.

In general, it is good advice for a solicitor to advise his client to remain silent, and there is nothing in any way unfair or underhand about this. On the assumption that your client is innocent (which the law presumes in his favour) his rights should be fully safeguarded, and it is his solicitor's duty to see that this is done. However, as with all rules, there are exceptions. Where your client has a clear defence, which he can substantiate, for example an alibi, it is in his interest to present it to the police at the earliest opportunity after it has been substantiated. Not only will this lend an air of consistency to any subsequent testimony by the defendant at trial, but it may result in further investigation which exonerates the client altogether before trial. If you are going to be present at your client's interrogation, and perhaps place him on even terms, you should consider whether the defence should be presented at an early stage. Do not, however, present any defence unless you have had sufficient opportunity to substantiate it, or where you require further instructions, or where legal research may be required. If in doubt, take advantage of the defendant's right to withhold his defence, until you are sure of your ground. In some cases, this will mean withholding until trial.

Where the defendant makes a statement to the police which tends to exculpate him, or is consistent with his defence, such statement is not a confession, and is inadmissible on the issue of guilt or innocence, because it is a self-serving statement. For the same reasons, if a statement is partly adverse and partly favourable then, on the issue of guilt or innocence, the adverse part is admissible but the self-serving part is inadmissible. A self-serving statement may be considered by the bench as evidence of consistency, if the defendant gives evidence, in that it shows his reaction when taxed with the offence, but this evidence goes to the defendant's credit as a witness only.

In some cases, the prosecution tender evidence of an interview which consists of a series of questions by the officer, followed by denials by the defendant. Because such an interview contains nothing of evidential value to the prosecution, but generally invites the court to listen to hearsay allegations communicated by the officer's questions, it is a proper and much under-used course to object to the admissibility of the interview. There is powerful authority of the House of Lords for such an application to exclude [30]. This does not apply where the nature or manner of the defendant's denials is probative of his guilt, for example where the defendant places his denial on a false basis, which the prosecution intend to disprove. However, such situations are exceptional, and do not affect the general rule.

Notes

1. In civil cases, the admissibility of adverse admissions is now governed by statute, the Civil Evidence Act 1968, s. 9.
2. *Deokinanan* v *R* [1969] 1 AC 20.
3. [1948] 1 All ER 794.
4. (1963) 48 Cr App R 116.
5. [1914] AC 599, 609.
6. In *DPP* v *Ping Lin* [1976] AC 574, 597–8, Lord Hailsham of St Marylebone pointed out that the word 'exercised' is probably a mis-rendering of 'excited', but added that the sense remained 'obvious and unaffected'.
7. *R* v *Smith* [1959] 2 QB 35, 39 per Lord Parker CJ.
8. *DPP* v *Ping Lin* [1976] AC 574.
9. *R* v *Davis* [1979] Crim LR 167.
10. *R* v *Kwabena Poku* [1978] Crim LR 488.
11. [1967] 1 AC 760, 820.

12. [1964] 1 QB 495, 501.
13. (1967) 51 Cr App R 1 n.
14. *R* v *May* (1952) 36 Cr App R 91; *R* v *Prager* [1972] 1 WLR 260.
15. [1977] 1 WLR 812, 816.
16. *R* v *Brackenbury* [1965] 1 WLR 1475 n; *Conway* v *Hotten* [1976] 2 All ER 213.
17. *R* v *Collier and Stenning* [1965] 1 WLR 1470.
18. [1977] 1 WLR 812.
19. The Criminal Law Act 1977, s. 62, introduced only a right to have one person notified of an arrest without unreasonable delay, and does not provide a statutory right of access to a solicitor while in custody.
20. [1971] 1 WLR 298, 301 per Lord Diplock.
21. *R* v *Osbourne*; *R* v *Virtue* [1973] QB 678.
22. *R* v *Dibble* (1908) 1 Cr App R 155.
23. *R* v *Rogers and Tarran* [1971] Crim LR 413; *R* v *Lake* (1976) 64 Cr App R 172.
24. *Turner* v *Underwood* [1948] 2 KB 284.
25. *R* v *Knight and Thompson* (1946) 31 Cr App R 52.
26. [1971] 1 WLR 298.
27. (1892) 17 Cox CC 503.
28. *Parkes* v *R* [1976] 1 WLR 1251.
29. *R* v *Chandler* [1976] 1 WLR 585.
30. *R* v *Christie* [1914] AC 545. See also *R* v *Norton* [1910] 2 KB 496.

Five

Evidence of Character

Introduction

This chapter is of primary, though not exclusive concern in criminal cases. There is probably no criminal case in which the defendant's character, be it good or bad, does not pose some problem for the advocate. Usually, the problems are more on the defence side than the prosecution side, though this is by no means an invariable rule. Nor are the problems confined to cases in which the defendant's character is bad, though in such cases the problems differ from those in which his character is good. It is, therefore, a safe assumption that whether the defendant models his life-style on St Francis of Assisi or on Fagin, or on some representative of humanity somewhere between the two, his character will have to be considered in some detail.

Such consideration can be hampered by the client who will not tell even his own advocate the truth about his character, or who cannot remember all the painful details. It is always worth while spending time taking really detailed instructions about the defendant's previous convictions, since there are few things worse than having the true picture exposed for the first time in court. This process usually refreshes the defendant's memory, or brings home to him the futility of further disingenuity, as the case may be. But if he insists upon his version of events, do not be sceptical. In this age of computerised records, mistakes are alarmingly common, and the defendant may well be telling the truth. In such a case, you will need time to check the original court records. These instructions are essential at every stage of criminal proceedings—for bail applications, at trial and during mitigation, and the importance of taking them with great attention to detail cannot be overstated.

It is often assumed that the term 'character' refers only to previous convictions. But the existence of previous convictions is not the sum total of bad character, any more than their absence is the sum total of good character. Character, whether good or bad, comprises three distinct areas, all of which are the concern of the law of evidence. These are:

(a)   A person's general reputation in his community.
(b)   A person's propensity or disposition to behave in a certain way.
(c)   Previous specific acts, including but not limited to previous convictions.

In practice, the term 'character' is used to denote the existence or absence of previous convictions. Since the possession of previous convictions makes all the difference between good and bad character, the usage is harmless, as long as it is not allowed to obscure the wider meaning of the term.

This chapter is concerned with the extent to which evidence of each of these three matters may be introduced into evidence, or, if unfavourable, excluded. The simplest way to examine this subject is to analyse separately good and bad character in relation to the rules of evidence.

Good character

In representing a client of previous good character, it is fundamental to remember that evidence of his good character is not only admissible, but actually constitutes some evidence tending to show his innocence of the charge. This is a remarkable rule, since in the exceptional cases when evidence of bad character is admissible, such evidence affects only the credit of the defendant, and is not evidence of his guilt. The rule as to good character is one of fairness to the defendant, and was recently restated by the Court of Appeal in *R* v *Bryant*; *R* v *Oxley* [1]. The defendant, whose good character had been put before the jury, elected not to give evidence. The trial judge directed the jury that, since the defendant had not given evidence, his credit was not an issue and that accordingly the evidence of good character was irrelevant and should be disregarded. The Court of Appeal held this direction to be too restrictive. The evidence did not affect credit only, but operated to influence the jury to say 'whether they think it likely that a person with such a character would have

ommitted the offence'. The jury were therefore entitled to consider it
n the defendant's favour in any event. You can certainly argue to the
)ench that your client's good character makes it less likely that he
:ommitted the offence charged, although good advocacy dictates
·hat this argument should not be pressed too far; taken to absurd
·engths, it could suggest that no one should ever be convicted of a first
)ffence, and this the bench are unlikely to swallow.

Evidence of good character can be presented to the court in three
ways, which are acceptable individually or in combination, and all of
which should be used wherever possible. These are:

(a)   Cross-examination of the prosecution witnesses. The usual
·orm of this cross-examination is to elicit from the officer in charge of
·he case that the defendant has no previous convictions. The question
$hould be phrased specifically in terms of the absence of previous
:onvictions, and should not be a general enquiry about the
jefendant's 'good character'. The officer will have to concede a
jemonstrable absence of previous convictions, but he may be less
·helpful if he happens to think that good fortune in escaping
:onvictions in the past is the main foundation of your client's good
:haracter. Sometimes, other prosecution witnesses can give evidence
about your client's reputation in the community, though for obvious
·reasons you should be very sure of the likely answers before
embarking on such cross-examination; if such circumstances exist,
you can probably call your own character witness, which is much
safer.

(b)   Calling the defendant to give evidence and putting the
appropriate questions in chief. This is an auspicious introduction to
any evidence in chief, and should be dealt with at the outset, because
it puts everything else in perspective.

(c)   Calling character witnesses. The value of this is sadly
underestimated in modern trial practice. It is always worth asking the
defendant whether there is someone who can speak for him.
Preferably, this should be a person of standing in the community;
ministers of religion, professional persons and community leaders are
ideal, though employers and family are often more effective than is
popularly supposed. The fact that someone is prepared to attend
court and go into the witness-box to attest to your client's character is
a fact which compels the attention of almost every court.

The facts which may be proved in support of your client's good character are that he has no previous convictions, and that he is of good reputation in his community. Strictly speaking, the defendant may not introduce evidence of the personal opinion of a character witness about his character: *R* v *Rowton* [2]; or of previous specific creditable acts, such as handing in lost property at a police station; or of the defendant's general disposition to behave in certain ways: *R* v *Redgrave* [3]. For largely historical reasons, these latter facts are inadmissible, although this rule seems generally to be ignored in practice, either because it is not widely known or because of considerations of fairness to the defence.

When seeking to prove the defendant's good reputation within his community, you have the advantage that the concept of community is now given a broad meaning, rightly so in these days of widespread social mobility. Most courts will now accept that the proper term of reference is the defendant's own circle, which need not be a strictly geographic circle in the old neighbourhood sense, but may be a social, professional, ethnic or other appropriate circle; good reputation is a positive fact in any of these contexts. The proper method of questioning a character witness is therefore: 'Are you aware of what people generally in [describe the circle] think of the [the defendant] with respect to honesty or dishonesty?', and 'What is the general opinion of [the defendant] within this circle?' The first of these questions is essential foundation for the second.

From a prosecution standpoint, apart from any objection to the inadmissible facts referred to above, the main area of concern is the case in which the defendant falsely states that he is of good character, whereas in fact he has previous convictions. The existence of previous convictions is the only area in which good character can be refuted effectively. Trying to refute an assertion of good reputation is like trying to punch a sponge, unless you happen to have a character witness who is unaware that the defendant has previous convictions. Where the defendant misrepresents his character to the court, the prosecution are in an enviable position, even where the misrepresentation is unintentional, as can be the case. If this happens, the prosecution have two weapons available:

(a) Cross-examination of the defendant. Unlike any other witness, the defendant giving evidence for the defence in a criminal trial enjoys a general immunity against being cross-examined about his bad character or previous convictions. This immunity was conferred by s. 1 of the Criminal Evidence Act 1898, the statute which first made the defendant a competent witness for the defence. The immunity is usually described as the defendant's 'shield'. The shield is created by s. 1(f) of the Act in the following terms:

> A person charged and called as a witness in pursuance of this Act shall not be asked, and if asked shall not be required to answer, any question tending to show that he has committed or been convicted of or been charged with any offence other than that wherewith he is then charged, or is of bad character.

The shield is not, however, absolute. In certain circumstances, the shield may be lost, with the result that the defendant becomes, like any other witness, liable to cross-examination about the generally prohibited matters. Each of the three sets of circumstances in which the shield may be lost will be considered in this chapter. This is the moment to deal with one of them. Section 1(f) continues:

> unless—. . .
> (ii)   he has personally or by his advocate asked questions of the witnesses for the prosecution with a view to establish his own good character, or has given evidence of his good character.

Determination of whether the effect of the defendant's cross-examination or evidence is such as to forfeit the shield is a matter of law for the bench, and it is improper to begin to cross-examine about character without asking the bench to rule, however obvious the matter may appear. There are cases in which it is genuinely doubtful whether the shield has been lost. It may be clear enough if the defendant gives evidence that he is a builder, and is hard-working, when such evidence can have no relevance to the case other than in terms of an assertion of good character. But what if the defendant asserts his trade in order to establish his innocent possession of apparent burglary tools? In such a case, any assertion of good character would seem to be no more than a necessary ancillary to proof of a relevant fact. Many courts and prosecutors would feel it to be unfair to cross-examine a defendant about his character in a case where he must deal with some aspect of his personal circumstances in order to give evidence in support of his defence, though regrettably, there are those who would seek to do so. A defence advocate may have to argue strongly that the shield has not been lost, if faced with such an unreasonable approach. It is good and professional for a prosecutor to recognise and act on the distinction between presentation of the defence and assertion of good character.

In conducting the cross-examination, it should be borne in mind that, although you can put the previous convictions to the defendant directly, and ask him about the sentences imposed and the general nature of the offences, it is not permissible to explore the detail of the previous offences so as to suggest guilt of the offence charged, even where the previous offences are similar in nature to the offence charged. The previous convictions are admissible only for the purpose of refuting the defendant's assertion of good character, and are not evidence of his guilt as charged: *R* v *France and France* [4]. This is not too much of a handicap, since the previous convictions are quite potent enough in their proper role. If you feel that the similarity between the offence charged and the previous offences is sufficiently compelling to be directly relevant to the issue of guilt as charged, you should be asking the court to rule that the previous convictions are admissible as similar-fact evidence, which is in no way dependent upon the question of whether or not the defendant asserts his good character. Similar-fact evidence is considered later in this chapter.

(b)   Cross-examination of a defendant is naturally possible only when the defendant has given evidence on which he may be cross-examined. It is not unknown for a defendant to suggest his asserted good character by cross-examination of the prosecution witnesses, or by calling a character witness, while exercising his right not to give evidence. In such a case, it seems that the prosecution would be entitled to call evidence in rebuttal, to demonstrate the defendant's true character. Although the authorities to this effect are cases in which the defendant avoided giving evidence by exercising the now abolished right to make an unsworn statement from the dock, the principle is unaffected. The leave of the court must be obtained by an application to adduce such evidence, but it should not be refused in any case where the defendant has misled the court with regard to his character.

Bad character

It is one of the fundamental principles of the English law of evidence that the prosecution may not adduce evidence of the defendant's previous bad character in order to prove his guilt of the offence charged. In English law, you cannot give a dog a bad name and hang it. The rule has never been better stated than in the following words of Lord Herschell LC in *Makin* v *Attorney-General for New South Wales* [5]:

> It is undoubtedly not competent for the prosecution to adduce evidence tending to show that the accused has been guilty of criminal acts other than those covered by the indictment, for the purpose of leading to the conclusion that the accused is a person likely from his criminal conduct or character to have committed the offence for which he is being tried.

This does not, of course, mean that there will be no occasion when the previous bad character of the defendant may be referred to in the course of the evidence. It means that the defendant's bad character may not, as such, be made part of the prosecution case against him. If the defendant is alleged to have assaulted a fellow prisoner while serving a sentence of imprisonment, the case cannot be presented without reference to the fact of the defendant's condition in life at the time of the offence. But evidence that the defendant was then a serving prisoner is not a use of his bad character to prove his guilt; it is simply necessary, relevant evidence of his guilt of the offence charged. The bench will not be told why he was in prison, because such evidence would be both irrelevant and inadmissible as evidence of bad character. The fact that he was in prison at the time of the offence is all that is relevant. The decision in *R* v *Chitson* [6] was dictated by similar considerations. The defendant was charged with unlawful sexual intercourse with girl 1. Girl 1 gave evidence that the defendant had boasted to her about his relationship with girl 2. Although the evidence of the boast about girl 2 arguably revealed that the defendant had committed a further offence, with which he was not then charged, the evidence was held to be admissible, because, if true, it supported the evidence of girl 1 about the circumstances in which the offence charged had taken place.

The above examples may be regarded as examples of relevant evidence which incidentally happens to reveal to the court some aspect of the bad character of the defendant. They are not cases in which the prosecution seek to use bad character as evidence of guilt.

Another and more specific example is to be found in what is termed similar-fact evidence. Similar-fact evidence is evidence of other acts, including but not limited to previous convictions, which are so strikingly similar in their nature to the facts of the offence charged that the court is justified in concluding that the similar features represent a hallmark of a particular offender, and that the same offender must have been responsible for each offence. In the rare cases where such a conclusion is justified, the evidence of similar acts is relevant to the issue of the defendant's guilt as charged. The degree of similarity required to make evidence of similar acts admissible is extremely high, simply because anything less would amount simply to evidence of bad character. Consequently, similar-fact evidence is rarely used, especially in the magistrates' court. It might have been omitted from this book altogether, were it not for a recent trend on the part of prosecutors to abuse the rule by seeking to introduce evidence of other acts which bear only a superficial similarity to the facts of the offence charged, for example evidence that the defendant stole goods of a similar nature during a previous shop-lifting expedition.

The degree of similarity required before evidence of similar acts becomes admissible was vividly illustrated by Lord Hailsham of St Marylebone in *DPP* v *Boardman* [7] using the following illustrations:

> Whilst it would certainly not be enough to identify the culprit in a series of burglaries that he climbed in through a ground-floor window, the fact that he left the same humorous limerick on the walls of the sitting-room, or an esoteric symbol written in lipstick on the mirror, might well be enough. In a sex case, to adopt an example given in argument in the Court of Appeal, whilst a repeated homosexual act by itself might be quite insufficient to admit the evidence as confirmatory of identity or design, the fact that it was alleged to have been performed wearing the ceremonial head-dress of a Red Indian chief or other eccentric garb might well in appropriate circumstances suffice.

No better example of the proper use of similar fact evidence could be imagined than that provided by the facts of one of the earliest of modern cases, *R* v *George Joseph Smith* [8], otherwise known to posterity as the 'brides-in-the-bath' case. The defendant was charged with the murder of a woman with whom he had gone through a ceremony of marriage. Evidence of the deaths of two other women, with whom the defendant had also gone through ceremonies of marriage, was held to have been rightly admitted. In each case, the deceased woman was found dead in her bath; in each case the door of the bathroom would not lock; in each case, the defendant had informed a doctor that the woman suffered from epileptic fits; and in each case, the woman's life was insured for the benefit of the defendant. The devastating degree of similarity in the different cases was not mere evidence of bad character, but was the clearest possible evidence of systematic crime, stamped with the hallmark of the individual defendant, from which the jury were justified in drawing the inference that each killing was murder, and murder by the same individual. But nothing short of this degree of similarity will do, for if the hallmark of the individual cannot be clearly shown, the evidence would be merely evidence of bad character, and not only inadmissible but so prejudicial as to make a fair trial almost impossible. Prosecutors should consider this with great care, before making any application to admit similar-fact evidence, and defence advocates should be vigilant to object to any apparent abuse of the rule.

Where relevant evidence incidentally involves the revelation of some aspect of the bad character of the defendant, the bench may not regard the incidentally revealed bad character as evidence of the guilt of the defendant as charged. But if the evidence is relevant, not only may the prosecution adduce such evidence as part of their case, they may also cross-examine the defendant about it, if he elects to give evidence. Section 1(e) of the Criminal Evidence Act 1898 provides:

A person charged and being a witness in pursuance of this Act may be asked any question in cross-examination notwithstanding that it would tend to criminate him as to the offence charged.

And s. 1(f) of the same Act, which created the shield of the defendant against cross-examination about his bad character, provides as its first exception that the defendant may be so cross-examined if:

(i) the proof that he has committed or been convicted of such other offence is admissible evidence to show that he is guilty of the offence wherewith he is then charged.

This might be the case where relevant evidence incidentally reveals some aspect of the defendant's bad character, or where similar-fact evidence is properly admissible.

Cross-examination about bad character

Section 1 of the Criminal Evidence Act 1898, which, for the first time, rendered the defendant a competent witness for the defence, invested the defendant witness with a shield against cross-examination about his bad character. The shield is not absolute, but may be lost in certain circumstances. We have considered the loss of the shield where the defendant asserts his own good character, and where cross-examination about character is relevant to the defendant's guilt of the offence charged. Two further situations in which the shield may be lost remain to be considered. These situations arise from the provisions of s. 1(f) that the defendant may be cross-examined about his character in either of the following two sets of circumstances, that is to say if:

> (ii) . . . the nature or conduct of the defence is such as to involve imputations on the character of the prosecutor or the witnesses for the prosecution;
> (iii) he [the defendant] has given evidence against any other person charged in the same proceedings.

These different cases must be considered separately.

Defences involving imputations on character

The defendant may make imputations on the character of the prosecutor or the witnesses for the prosecution either in the course of cross-examination (whether in person or by his advocate) or during the course of his evidence, or both. And unfortunately, unlike the case in the first part of s. 1(f)(ii) in which the defendant asserts his own good character, there may be little or nothing that you, as an advocate, can do to prevent loss of the shield. Some defences, by their very nature, involve making imputations on the character of the prosecutor or the witnesses for the prosecution. If the defendant is to be believed, the imputations may well be justified, but in any event you have a duty to make them if essential to the defence.

An imputation on character is any allegation which, if believed, a court would consider to be seriously discreditable to the witness. The most obvious examples are allegations that a prosecution witness has committed perjury, or fabricated evidence, for example where it is alleged that a police officer obtained a confession by force or fraud, or invented the contents of an interview. But any allegation of perjury, fabrication of evidence, serious misconduct or dishonest or immoral behaviour, including an imputation of criminal convictions, may suffice. Conversely a mere allegation of mistake or unreliability is insufficient to lose the shield. And where the defendant does no more than assert his innocence, even in strong terms, he does not lose his shield, even though the implication may be that the evidence against him is untrue. The shield is lost only by an express and affirmative allegation of some seriously discreditable conduct.

The mere fact that the making of imputations is inevitable, and is an essential part of the defence, is no answer to the loss of the shield. In *R* v *Bishop* [9], a defendant charged with burglary sought to show that he was not a trespasser in the building concerned by alleging that he had had a homosexual relationship with the occupier. Clearly, this was no more than a necessary part of the defence, and was designed not to attack the character of the occupier, but to refute an essential element of the offence charged, by suggesting that the defendant had permission to enter the building and so was not a trespasser. The shield was nonetheless lost.

The advocate does, however, retain a certain degree of control, in that it may be possible to conduct the defence without recourse to the making of imputations on character. This will occur where the 'nature' of the defence does not necessarily involve imputations, but the 'conduct' of the defence may or may not involve them, depending upon the manner in which it is undertaken. As an advocate, you should not make an imputation on the character of any witness, unless you are credibly instructed that the imputation can be made, and unless it is essential to the conduct of the defence. The first 'unless' represents a rule of professional conduct; the second represents a rule of professional judgment, in the sense that it is a cardinal error to throw away your client's shield without good reason. In certain cases, you will have absolutely no choice but to suffer the loss of the shield, since the very essence of your defence may be that the prosecution witnesses are lying, or have fabricated evidence against your client. The tactical implications of this, and one method of minimising the damage, are considered in Chapter 10.

The purpose of permitting cross-examination about character in such circumstances is that the court is entitled to evaluate the attack made on the prosecution witnesses in the light of the character of the person who makes it. An imputation on character will carry more weight if it emanates from a defendant of good character, than if it emanates from a defendant with numerous previous convictions. For this reason, even where the shield is lost, the evidence of the defendant's bad character is admissible only as evidence of the defendant's credit as the author of the imputations, and may not be used as evidence of his guilt.

In the Crown Court, the judge has power to restrain the cross-examination permitted, either by excluding it altogether, or by limiting it to certain aspects of the defendant's character, on the ground that exposure of character would unduly prejudice the defendant's right to a fair trial: *Selvey* v *DPP* [10]. Even if this power may be exercised by magistrates, which has been doubted, it is self-defeating, in the sense that even to ask for the exercise of the discretion gives the game away. This does not mean, however, that the prosecution should proceed to cross-examine without asking leave. As in the case where the defendant asserts his good character, the bench must determine, as a matter of law, that the shield has been lost before the cross-examination is proper.

Giving evidence against co-defendants

Section 1(f)(iii) removes the shield in cross-examination not by the prosecution, but by co-defendants. It is comparatively simple to determine when the shield has been lost in these circumstances, although this too is a question of law for the bench, and leave to cross-examine is required. In the Crown Court, the difference is that the judge has no power to restrain cross-examination by a co-defendant if the shield is lost as a matter of law.

A defendant 'gives evidence against' another, if he gives evidence which assists the prosecution case against the other, or undermines the other's defence, in either case making it more likely that the other will be convicted: *R* v *Bruce and others* [11]. This does not mean that the defendant must testify as a prosecution witness against the co-defendant; indeed, he is an incompetent witness for this purpose. What is envisaged is the by no means uncommon situation in which a defendant will seek, during his evidence in chief on his own behalf, to inculpate a co-defendant, in order to exculpate himself. However, he need not give evidence with that intention; if his evidence in fact has the required detrimental effect on the co-defendant's case, the shield is lost: *Murdoch* v *Taylor* [12].

'Any other person charged in the same proceedings' means any other person also charged and before the court in the same trial, even though the charges against that co-defendant may not be identical to those against the defendant witness.

As in the case of imputations against prosecution witnesses, there are many cases in which loss of the shield is inevitable. However, good advocacy demands that the shield should not be lost unnecessarily, where the defendant's case does not call for an assault on the defence of co-defendants. Also similar to the rule in the case of imputations on character is the principle that, since the object of the permitted cross-examination is to allow the court to assess the weight to be attached to the evidence against the co-defendant by reference to the character of the defendant witness, the evidence of bad character is evidence only of the credit of the defendant witness as the author of the evidence adverse to the co-defendant, and is not evidence of the guilt of the defendant witness.

Improper references to character

A reference during a criminal trial to the previous bad character of a defendant, other than when permitted by the rules of evidence, is a serious irregularity. The proper course for a defence advocate, unless he intends for the tactical reasons outlined in Chapter 10 to introduce his client's character anyway, or it is inevitable that the shield will be lost at a later stage, is to apply immediately for a retrial before a differently constituted bench. The prejudice that may otherwise operate against the defendant, even though the bench may be fair-minded and may try to exclude the reference from their minds, may preclude a fair trial, and will almost certainly preclude the appearance of a fair trial.

Improper references to character can occur in various ways, by inadvertence or malevolence from the mouth of a prosecution witness or co-defendant, or through a mistake on the part of the defendant himself. Of these, the last is the most embarrassing possibility. However, even in this case, a properly advised bench should grant the retrial, particularly where the answer which reveals character has been induced by cross-examination. The only exception is where the defendant, seeing his defence coming apart at the seams, deliberately sabotages the trial by an unprovoked revelation of his past record. This is a mercifully rare occurrence.

Oddly enough, there are situations even more embarrassing than the voluntary disclosure of bad character by the defendant. These are situations where the defendant's advocate invites an improper reference to character in the course of cross-examination of the prosecution witnesses. If this seems unlikely, consider the effect of questions such as the following:

(a) 'Why were you following my client?'

(b) 'What exactly was being discussed at the police station, while you were not interviewing my client about this offence?'

(c) 'How did you know my client's name when you first saw him on the street?'

(d) 'What did my client tell you that you have not given in evidence today?'

If these questions have one thing in common, it is that they are questions which defendants often urge you to put. If they have a second thing in common, it is that they are all potentially disastrous, for even though the answers may be inadmissible, it is no use objecting after they have been given, when you yourself have induced them. The bench will assume that you have some good reason for doing so. A good advocate will sense that he is straying into dangerous territory, merely by the fact that the police officer has (following his training better than some advocates follow theirs) stayed carefully away from the subject in chief, and exhibits an embarrassed reluctance to answer in cross-examination. The latter is often mistaken by the inexperienced advocate as a sign of evasion, with terrible results. Pressed far enough, the officer will tell the court what he knows.

Finally, it should be noted that the Rehabilitation of Offenders Act 1974 and the Children and Young Persons Act 1963, s. 16(2), provide some restriction on the disclosure of certain previous convictions that occurred long ago, or while a person was a child or young person. In the case of the former statute, the restriction is only one of first obtaining leave before referring to a spent conviction in open court, for the Act does not apply to references during criminal proceedings [13]. The latter prohibits the disclosure of the covered offences in any event. Quite apart from these restrictions, a wise prosecutor will often refrain from dredging up ancient convictions even though he may technically be entitled to do so, especially where the defendant's recent record is good. Quite often, such an error of judgment forfeits the sympathy of the court and transfers it to the defendant, and accomplishes nothing in terms of attacking the defendant's credit.

Notes

1. [1979] QB 108.
2. (1865) Le & Ca 520.
3. (1981) 74 Cr App R 10.
4. [1979] Crim LR 48.
5. [1894] AC 57, 65.
6. [1909] 2 KB 945.
7. [1975] AC 421, 454.
8. [1915] 11 Cr App R 229.
9. [1975] QB 274.
10. [1970] AC 304.
11. [1975] 1 WLR 1252.
12. [1965] AC 574.
13. Practice Direction (Queen's Bench Division) (Crime: Spent convictions) [1975] 1 WLR 1065.

Six

Witnesses

Introduction

In Chapter 1, it was said that there are different varieties of evidence which may be presented to a court. Oral evidence is one of these varieties, and it is presented to the court by witnesses. Chapters 8 and 10 will say much more about the actual evidence which witnesses may give, and about the preparation and presentation of evidence given in chief, in cross-examination and in re-examination. This chapter examines some very basic questions about witnesses which are often overlooked in the course of concentrating on the substance of the witnesses' evidence. These are questions affecting the witnesses themselves, as distinguished from the evidence which they may give. Because witnesses are the foundation of almost every contested case, an understanding of the rules that affect them is a basic tool of advocacy.

In order to study these rules concerning witnesses, we shall try to answer four questions which you should ask, namely:

(a) What witnesses can I call to give evidence?
(b) What witnesses can I compel to attend to give evidence?
(c) What kinds of witnesses should I call to give evidence?
(d) How many witnesses should I call to give evidence?

What witnesses can I call to give evidence?

This question focuses, not upon the actual evidence that a witness may be able to give, but upon the personal qualification or disqualification of a witness to be called to give evidence at all. A person who is personally qualified to give evidence is said to be 'competent' and one who is disqualified on personal grounds, to be 'incompetent'. To the modern mind, the idea that any witness should be incompetent to give evidence seems rather strange, given that the court should have access to as much relevant evidence as possible, and certainly, the court will favour competency wherever incompetency can properly be avoided. But, as in so many instances, the rules of evidence regarding competence remain shackled to some extent by their historical development.

At common law, there were a number of general incompetences, based on the premise that there were certain persons whose evidence must always be too suspect or unreliable to be accepted by a court, for example, persons convicted of infamous crimes and non-Christians. But the common law also recognised specific incompetences, which arose from the relationship of a person to the case in question. The parties to a case and their spouses were incompetent because of their personal interest in the outcome. The general incompetences based on character or inability to take the prescribed oath have long since been abolished by statute, and general incompetence is now significant only with respect to the evidence of children of tender years, and persons of defective intellect. The specific incompetences affecting the parties and their spouses likewise survive only in a much emasculated form, and only in relation to criminal cases. In civil cases, the parties and their spouses have long been competent by statute.

We shall look first at the specific incompetences of the defendant and the spouse of the defendant in criminal cases, and then turn to the general incompetence affecting children of tender years and persons of defective intellect.

Defendants in criminal cases   At common law, the defendant in a criminal case was, like any other party, incompetent to give evidence. In an age of harsh punishments and frequent denial of counsel, this incompetence gradually came to be regarded as unjust and it was eventually removed by s. 1 of the Criminal Evidence Act 1898. The Act provided that:

> Every person charged with an offence . . . shall be a competent witness for the defence at every stage of the proceedings, whether the person so charged is charged solely or jointly with any other person.

This section still forms the basis of the right of the defendant to go into the witness-box in his defence, in any criminal trial, whether summary or on indictment. Note that the phrase 'at every stage of the proceedings' is broad enough to encompass the right to give evidence not only at trial, but also in ancillary proceedings such as applications for bail and committal proceedings and in mitigation of sentence: *R* v *Wheeler* [1].

Whenever a defendant does give evidence in his defence as permitted by the Act, the bench must weigh his evidence as they would that of any other witness. It is always proper, and often desirable to remind the bench in tactful terms that they should not view his evidence with suspicion merely because he moves from the dock to the witness-box to give it. The Act, incidentally, gives the defendant the right to give evidence from the witness-box, unless the court otherwise orders: s. 1(g). The court may so order only in a case of necessity, for example where the defendant is of violent disposition and may be difficult to control: *R* v *Symonds* [2].

Because s. 1 makes the defendant a competent witness 'for the defence' and not just on his own personal behalf, he may (with his consent) be called as a witness by a co-defendant. However, since he would thereby subject himself to cross-examination about the case as a whole, including his own involvement, it is difficult to imagine a case in which he would consent to be called for a co-defendant, having declined to be called by his own advocate.

The Act renders the defendant a competent witness only for the defence. It is important to note that the defendant remains incompetent as a witness for the prosecution: *R* v *Grant* [3]. For various reasons, it is usually the hope of the prosecution that the defendant will give evidence. The prosecution cannot require a reluctant defendant A to go into the witness-box to give evidence in his own defence, for the Act precludes any such compulsion. But can the prosecution call a willing defendant A to give evidence for them against co-defendant B? Defendant A's motive for such treachery might be the hope of attracting a more lenient sentence, or the expectation that the prosecution might play down his involvement in the case, at the expense of defendant B. Whatever the motive on either side, it cannot be done while A is a defendant in the case; he is incompetent for the prosecution.

Of course, if defendant A ceases to be a defendant, because he is no longer a person charged and before the court, his incompetence is removed. This will be the case if he has pleaded guilty to all the charges against him, or the prosecution decide not to proceed with any charges to which he has not pleaded guilty, or not to proceed against him at all. Where the prosecution propose to call such a witness, the situation requires delicate handling by all the advocates in the case. Even though he may thus become a competent prosecution witness, A's credit as a witness is open to powerful challenge, and his evidence will almost always require corroboration because he is likely to be an accomplice in the offences charged.

A's credit as a witness can be protected to some extent if the bench are prepared to sentence A before the trial proceeds against B. This can take some of the steam out of the inevitable cross-examination about his motive for giving evidence for the prosecution. Having received a reasonably lenient sentence, A may prove less enthusiastic in his evidence on behalf of the prosecution. Nonetheless if you are defending B, your position is generally rendered somewhat easier if sentence is deferred until the end of the trial. In this case, it may be easier to ensure by cross-examination that the bench understand that A has something to gain by giving evidence against B, or at least believes that he has something to gain. As to the correct moment at which to sentence a former defendant whom the prosecution require as a witness, fashion varies. Often, however, the bench will accept that they do not have enough facts to sentence A fairly before the respective roles of A and B have been fully explored. There are no limitations on the magistrates' freedom to choose which course to follow.

The defendant's spouse   As in the case of the defendant himself, the questions affecting the defendant's spouse in a criminal case are whether or not the spouse is a competent witness for the prosecution, and whether or not the spouse is a competent witness for the defence. The latter is the simpler question, and may be dealt with conveniently first.

At common law, the spouses of the parties to a case were incompetent to the same extent, and for the same reasons, as the parties themselves. Consequently, when the Criminal Evidence Act 1898 removed the incompetence of the defendant as a witness for the defence, it was logical that the incompetence of the spouse should likewise be removed, and this was done. We have already looked at s. 1 of the Act, in so far as it refers to the defendant. The full text of the section, incorporating proviso (c), also sets forth the Act's provisions with regard to spouses:

> Every person charged with an offence, and the wife or husband, as the case may be, of the person so charged, shall be a competent witness for the defence at every stage of the proceedings, whether the person so charged is charged solely or jointly with any other person. Provided as follows: . . .
>
> (c) The wife or husband of the person charged shall not, save as in this Act mentioned, be called as a witness in pursuance of this Act except upon the application of the person so charged.

The phrase 'save as in this Act mentioned' refers to s. 4 and the schedule to the Act, which render the spouse a competent witness for the prosecution in certain limited cases. While creating a general competence in the spouse as a defence witness, the Act, by proviso (c), ensures that it is the decision of the defendant, not that of the spouse, which governs whether the spouse will be called.

The spouse as a witness for the prosecution presents more difficult problems. The rule is, technically, that the spouse of the defendant is not a competent witness for the prosecution, though it is a rule which has almost been swallowed up by exceptions. The common law, basing itself mainly on the unity of husband and wife and the undesirability of spouses testifying against each other, held the spouse to be incompetent. But even at common law, exceptional cases were recognised.

The important common-law exception is in the case of offences of violence by one spouse against the other, or against a member of the family. The limits of the exception were never exactly defined. As long ago as *Lord Audley's case* [4], it was clear that it applied to serious offences of violence. *Audley's case* involved a charge of aiding and abetting rape on a wife. But it remained unclear until comparatively recently whether the exception also applied to cases where no actual violence ensued, for example an attempt to murder the wife. In *R* v *Verolla* [5] this question was answered in the affirmative. It still remains unclear whether any particular degree of violence, or closeness of relationship is required. Fortunately, statutory intervention has probably rendered these considerable areas of uncertainty less critical.

The law has developed much more rapidly by way of statutory exception, beginning with the Criminal Evidence Act 1898. From a prosecutor's standpoint, it is easier and more satisfactory to be able to point to some specific statutory justification for calling a spouse, than to rely on the uncertain ambit of the common law. The modern statutory provisons, particularly the Theft Act 1968, s. 30, are broad enough to apply to a wide variety of offences. But there are cases where the common law must still be resorted to, and it should always be borne in mind where an offence of violence against a member of the family is charged.

The statutory exceptions are contained mainly in the Criminal Evidence Act 1898, s. 4, and the schedule to the Act as amended, the Sexual Offences Act 1956, s. 39, and the Theft Act 1968, s. 30. More specific provisions are sometimes found in other statutes, for example the Indecency with Children Act 1960. With the exception of the Theft Act 1968, which must be considered separately, all these provisions relate to specific offences, or categories of offences, which broadly speaking affect the physical welfare of the family. In dealing with a statutory offence which has such characteristics, the statute creating the offence, together with the Criminal Evidence Act 1898 and the Sexual Offences Act 1956, should always be checked for such a provision.

It is s. 30 of the Theft Act 1968 which has affected the competence of the spouse most dramatically. The section was hidden away in a statute passed to create a new body of substantive law dealing with offences of dishonesty, and considering this, the potential breadth of the provision is startling:

(2)   . . . a person shall have the same right to bring proceedings against that person's wife or husband for any offence (whether under this Act or otherwise) as if they were not married, and a person bringing any such proceedings shall be competent to give evidence for the prosecution at every stage of the proceedings.

(3)   Where a person is charged in proceedings not brought by that person's wife or husband with having committed any offence with reference to that person's wife or husband or to property belonging to the wife or husband, the wife or husband shall be competent to give evidence at every stage of the proceedings, whether for the defence or for the prosecution, and whether the accused is charged solely or jointly with any other person.

The scope of subsection (3) in particular may provide an answer for prosecutors in any case where the application of the common-law exception or narrower statutory exceptions is in doubt. The section is not confined to offences under the Act itself, and the phrase 'with reference to that person's wife or husband or to property belonging to the wife or husband' is clearly wider than any provision dealing with offences committed 'against' the spouse. It includes any offence which affects the rights or obligations of a spouse. For example, in *R* v *Noble* [6], a husband was held to be a competent witness on the prosecution of his wife for forgery of his signature on documents submitted to a finance company. Since the finance company would not have considered a loan application backed only by the signature of the wife, the husband's rights and obligations under the transaction were affected by the wife's act of forgery.

It would be unrealistic, in this day and age, to leave the subject of the competence of spouses without referring to the position of former spouses, and of cohabitees, 'common-law wives' and the like. One of the few advantages of lawful wedlock over cohabitation is that it renders one's spouse incompetent as a prosecution witness against one. A cohabitee, by whatever name he or she may be known, is not a 'spouse' for the purpose of the competence rule, and is accordingly competent in all cases.

For the same reasons, if the defendant and the proposed witness are in fact lawfully married, the spouse witness remains incompetent even though the parties to the marriage may be separated. A spouse remains a spouse, whether or not cohabiting with his or her partner, and it matters not whether the separation is pursuant to a separation agreement or to an order of the court. Even after divorce, the rule in criminal cases is that a spouse remains incompetent to give evidence of any matters that occurred during the subsistence of the marriage, though as to matters occurring subsequently the position is naturally otherwise, since those same parties are no longer spouses. In *R* v *Algar* [7], the defendant was charged with forgery of his wife's signature on cheques drawn on her bank account during 1947 and 1948. In 1949, the marriage was annulled because of the impotence of the defendant (a ground which rendered the marriage voidable only, and not void *ab initio*). At the defendant's trial in 1953, the former wife was called as a witness. Quashing the conviction, the Court of Criminal Appeal held that she had been incompetent, and that her evidence had been wrongly admitted. Were the facts to recur now, the wife would probably be held to be competent under s. 30(3) of the Theft Act 1968.

Children of tender years   The competence or incompetence of children is determined not on a class basis, as for defendants or spouses, but with reference to the maturity and understanding of the individual child. The test, in broad terms, is whether the child has sufficient understanding of the duty to tell the truth and is sufficiently capable of giving comprehensible evidence to justify the reception of his or her evidence, given the danger of fabrication, exaggeration or capriciousness. A child whose competence is in doubt because of age or ability to fulfil these conditions is generally referred to as a child of tender years.

The question is not simply one of age, though age is, of course, an important factor. The question is whether the court is satisfied of the child's ability to appreciate the nature of the proceedings and the duty to tell the truth, and of the child's reliability as a witness. It is imperative that, before permitting a child of tender years to give evidence, the court ask questions of the child in open court, with a view to satisfying itself of the child's competence.

The test was stated by the Court of Appeal in *R* v *Hayes* [8] as follows:

> The important consideration, we think, when a judge has to decide whether a child should properly be sworn, is whether the child has a sufficient appreciation of the solemnity of the occasion and the added responsibility to tell the truth, which is involved in taking an oath, over and above the duty to tell the truth which is an ordinary duty of normal social conduct.

If the court is not satisfied that a child is competent to give sworn evidence, there is still one further avenue of approach open. In the days before *R* v *Hayes*, Parliament had recognised that mere inability to be sworn should not necessarily keep a child's evidence from a court. By s. 38(1) of the Children and Young Persons Act 1933 it was enacted that:

> Where, in any proceedings against any person for an offence, any child of tender years called as a witness does not in the opinion of the court understand the nature of an oath, his evidence may be

received, though not given upon oath, if, in the opinion of the court, he is possessed of sufficient intelligence to justify the reception of the evidence, and understands the duty of speaking the truth.

The subsection corresponds very closely with the modern test for the reception of sworn evidence as propounded in *R* v *Hayes*. In most cases, therefore, where the court is of the opinion that the child is competent to give unsworn evidence under s. 38(1), it should be persuaded that he or she is competent to give sworn evidence. In a marginal case, however, you will sometimes find that the court will accept unsworn, but not sworn evidence. Unsworn evidence is better than no evidence at all, and in many cases is just as compelling as evidence given on oath. However, it should be remembered that where unsworn evidence is given for the prosecution, the proviso to the subsection provides that the defendant 'shall not be liable to be convicted of the offence unless that evidence is corroborated by some other material evidence in support thereof implicating him'.

Quite apart from questions of competence, the treatment of child witnesses is one of the most delicate and demanding tasks that can face an advocate, particularly in sexual cases. The potential for alienating the bench is never greater than in the context of a decision of whether or not to call a child, or of how to cross-examine a child. The task of the defence advocate is especially demanding, because regardless of the important considerations of the physical and mental welfare of the child, the advocate must not forget that hysterical invention and exaggeration are a real possibility in the evidence of a young child. For this reason alone, a defence advocate should insist that the court be satisfied about the child's competence. Once the court is so satisfied, there can be no objection to a thorough and testing cross-examination, provided that it is conducted with restraint and tact.

As a prosecutor, you should ensure that a responsible adult attends court with the child, and that the child is physically and mentally fit to give evidence. Your examination-in-chief should be as short as is consistent with your duty to elicit the facts. As a defender, you must put your client's case fully, but you should vary your style of cross-examination from that which you might employ in the case of an adult witness. Bear in mind that you can emphasise to the court in your closing speech the dangers of the evidence of children. You need not make all your points in cross-examination, and it is usually unnecessary to drive home points of inconsistency or weakness at this stage. The bench will be receptive to them during your closing speech, and will appreciate your restraint and consideration in reserving them until that time.

Both sides should bear in mind the important statutory provisions dealing with the evidence of child witnesses in committal proceedings, contained in ss. 42 and 43 of the Children and Young Persons Act 1933 and s. 103 of the Magistrates' Courts Act 1980, and designed to reduce as far as possible the ordeal involved in giving evidence which will be repeated at the trial on indictment.

Persons of defective intellect   Witnesses whose intellectual powers are diminished for any reason are competent to the extent that the court is satisfied that they understand the nature of the proceedings and the duty to tell the truth, and are capable of giving comprehensible evidence. Many witnesses can assist the court with relevant facts, despite some degree of mental handicap. If necessary, the court may adjourn the case in order for the witness to recover his or her capacity. This is sometimes done in the case of witnesses who are suffering from temporary mental incapacity caused by alcohol or drugs. The court will permit any witness to give evidence whenever possible (unless outraged by any self-induced incapacity) although the weight of the evidence given may not be great.

What witnesses can I compel to attend to give evidence?

The general rule in both civil and criminal cases is that any witness who is competent to give evidence is also compellable to do so. By compellable is meant that the witness may be lawfully required by the court, under penalty of sanction for refusal to obey, to attend and give evidence. The purpose of the rule is to prevent the court from being deprived of relevant evidence, merely because of the refusal of a witness to co-operate. However, for reasons which have already been explored in this chapter, when discussing competence, there are exceptions in the cases of a defendant and the spouse of a defendant in a criminal case.

Section 1 of the Criminal Evidence Act 1898, which for the first time made a defendant and his or her spouse competent witnesses for the defence, provided that the defendant should not be called as a witness 'except on his own application', and that the spouse should not be called as a witness for the defence 'except on the application of the person . . . charged'. It is clear from the wording of the section that the defendant is not a compellable witness. It follows that the defendant need never give evidence unless he wishes to do so, and the question of whether it may ever be advisable not to call the defendant is dealt with in Chapter 10. It should be noted, however, that if the defendant does elect to give evidence, he becomes a witness and his evidence becomes evidence for all purposes in the case, and he cannot object to being cross-examined on behalf of the prosecution and any co-defendants, once he has been sworn.

It is now settled that the defendant's spouse is never compellable for the prosecution, even in the exceptional cases where he or she may be a competent prosecution witness: *Hoskyn* v *Commissioner of Police for the Metropolis* [9].

When dealing with the spouse of a defendant, it is also worth bearing in mind that there is a privilege in criminal cases which protects a spouse to whom matrimonial communications are made from being compelled to divulge them in evidence. Section 3 of the Evidence Amendment Act 1853 provides that:

No husband shall be compellable to disclose any communication made to him by his wife during the marriage, and no wife shall be compellable to disclose any communication made to her by her husband during the marriage [10].

Merely to know whether a witness is compellable is not enough. Prosecuting and defending advocates alike should be familiar with the procedure in the magistrates' court for compelling the attendance of witnesses, by applying before trial to the court for the issuance of a witness summons: Magistrates' Courts Act 1980, s. 97(1). The summons, which may be issued by the clerk to the justices as well as the justices themselves, is available in any case where the bench or clerk is satisfied that any person in England or Wales is likely to be able to give material evidence, or produce any document or thing likely to be material evidence, and that the person will not voluntarily attend as a witness or produce the document or thing. The summons directs the witness to attend before the court at the time and date stated, to give evidence or to produce the document or thing. The witness summons must be served personally on the witness, and the compelling party must tender with the summons a sum of money reasonably sufficient to defray the witness's expenses involved in attending.

By s. 97(2) of the Magistrates' Courts Act 1980, if a justice of the peace (not the clerk in this instance) is satisfied by evidence on oath that it is probable that a witness summons would be insufficient to procure the attendance of the witness, the justice may issue a warrant to arrest the witness and bring him before the court. This is a drastic step, and justices are likely to grant this relief only where it appears strictly necessary, for example where the witness has already failed to obey a witness summons. Furthermore, if the witness attends, but refuses without just cause to be sworn or to give evidence, or to produce the document or object, the court has power to commit him to custody for up to seven days or until he sooner complies with the order of the court.

In the county court, a witness summons may also be issued on the request of a party under CCR Ord. 20, r. 12, for the attendance of a witness or the production of any document or object. Failure to obey the summons may be visited by a fine as provided for by the County Courts Act 1959, s. 84.

When one looks at the available procedure, it is surprising that one so often hears advocates complaining that their cases are being hindered by reluctant witnesses. Having said that, there will be occasions when, as a matter of professional judgment, you will decide not to call a reluctant witness. The mere fact that the power to compel exists does not mean that it is tactically correct to make use of it in every case. There will be cases in which the witness's evidence will be so affected by his reluctance or hostility that it would be too dangerous to call him. On the other hand, there will also be cases in which the witness's evidence is of great importance to your case, and where it would be irresponsible not to make use of the power to compel. Even though a witness may have expressed reluctance to attend court, this may amount to no more than a natural disinclination to take time off work and spend a good part of a day waiting around a magistrates' or county court. Service of a witness summons often reminds a witness of his civic duties, and you will often find that, when presented with a document to show to his employer, the witness may suddenly find that he is not quite as reluctant to take a day off work as he initially appeared. If in doubt, always have the witness attend. You do not have to call the witness merely because he is at court (though bear in mind that the other side may do so) but his presence gives you an opportunity to assess his mood.

How many witnesses should I call to give evidence?

The number of witnesses to be called is almost always governed by an advocate's tactical and professional judgment. In some instances, it is governed by his or her duty as a prosecutor. In a relatively few situations, it is governed by the rules of law concerning corroboration. The last-named cases are few in number, since the rule of English law is that any case may be proved by the evidence of one witness, in the absence of some specific rule to the contrary. We shall therefore look first at the judgmental considerations, including the duty of the prosecution to call witnesses, and then at the rules of corroboration.

Considerations of judgment   The days of compurgators are long gone. Modern advocacy does not depend on the number of witnesses called on one side or the other. Of course, if two or more credible witnesses corroborate each other, that is to say support each other's evidence, then of course the weight of their combined evidence is likely to be greater than the uncorroborated evidence of either. It is, therefore, safe to state that you should call all the credible, available evidence that supports your case. But this should not be taken as an absolute rule. There is no substitute for professional judgment in this matter, any more than in any other aspect of successful advocacy. If one witness has accurately and forcibly given evidence of the relevant facts, and has emerged unshaken from cross-examination, you will not necessarily wish to risk losing some of the impact of that evidence by calling a less impressive witness to repeat the same evidence. Sometimes, a client will present you with a number of witnesses whose very availability in quantity should arouse your suspicion. You are not obliged to call them all. Any court will find its suspicions aroused on seeing a veritable procession of friends and relatives of the defendant, or any party, follow each other into the witness-box in quick succession to say exactly the same thing.

For prosecutors, the above principles are modified to some extent by the duty of the prosecution to see that a fair trial is had, so far as possible. This does not mean that the prosecution should not also seek to make their case as persuasive as possible, and it is certainly within the discretion of a prosecutor not to call a witness who appears not to be credible. However, it is a general rule that the prosecution should either call or make available at court all witnesses from whom the prosecution have taken a statement, even though their evidence may not support the prosecution case, and may even be inconsistent with the prosecution case: *R* v *Bryant* [11]. Calling a witness does not necessarily mean eliciting his evidence in chief: in the prosecutor's discretion, the witness may be sworn and then tendered for cross-examination. There is no duty on the prosecution to supply the defence with the witness's statement.

Requirements for corroboration　In a limited number of cases, the question of how many witnesses to call is decided in part by rules requiring corroboration. It should be emphasised once again that these cases are exceptional, since the basic rule of law is that a court may act on the evidence of a single witness, even for the purpose of convicting of a criminal charge. But because certain kinds of evidence are perceived to be inherently dangerous or unreliable, because of the source of the evidence or the presumed characteristics of the witness, the law sometimes requires corroboration before a conviction may be obtained, or requires the court to warn itself of the potential danger of convicting on the basis of uncorroborated evidence.

Corroboration means no more than that a piece of evidence (the evidence to be corroborated) is supported or confirmed by another piece of evidence (the corroborating evidence). When one piece of evidence supports and confirms another, and the court accepts both, the first piece of evidence is said to be corroborated by the second.

In order to be capable of being corroborative, evidence must (a) be admissible in itself, (b) emanate from a source independent of the evidence to be corroborated, and (c) be such as to tend to show, by confirmation of some material particular, not only that the offence charged was committed, but also that the defendant committed it.

The reason for the use of the phrase 'capable of being corroborative' is that in dealing with corroboration, the bench must deal with two questions. The first, which is one of law, is whether the evidence tendered as corroboration is capable of constituting corroboration, so that the evidence is potentially corroborative. This question is answered by reference to whether it meets the three requirements set forth above. The second, which is one of fact, is whether the bench accept the evidence, so that it in fact becomes corroborative. In the magistrates' court, the bench must answer both questions.

Cases in which corroboration must be considered are of two classes. The first class, described as cases where corroboration is required as a matter of law, comprises specific statutory instances in which a conviction cannot, as a matter of law, be obtained unless corroboration is available of the evidence requiring it. The second, and more general class, described as cases where corroboration is to be looked for as a matter of practice, comprises those cases in which the bench may convict on uncorroborated evidence, but must first warn themselves of the danger of so doing.

The first class is based on various specific, statutory provisons, and need not detain us for long, but should always be borne in mind during a perusal of statutory provisions when considering an unfamiliar statutory offence. Examples of statutory requirements for corroboration as a matter of law are speeding, personation at a general or municipal election and various offences of procuring the defilement of women and girls and procuring women and girls for the purpose of prostitution. To depart from the criminal sphere for a moment, it is also worth observing that a finding of paternity under s. 4(2) of the Affiliation Proceedings Act 1957 as amended, requires corroboration of the evidence of the mother implicating the defendant in an act of sexual intercourse with her at about the time of conception: *Cracknell* v *Smith* [12].

Finally, as has already been said, the unsworn evidence of a child of tender years, given under s. 38(1) of the Children and Young Persons Act 1933, must be corroborated, if the defendant is to be convicted. The unsworn evidence of a child cannot be corroborated by the unsworn evidence of another child given under the same subsection. However, the sworn evidence of the second child may be corroborative of the unsworn evidence of the first: *DPP* v *Hester* [13].

The second class requires consideration of three different kinds of evidence which are regarded at common law as being inherently suspicious or dangerous. These are: (a) the sworn evidence of children of tender years, (b) the evidence of accomplices and (c) the evidence of complainants of sexual misconduct.

(a) Children. Just as there is no set age beyond which a child becomes automatically competent, so there is no set age beyond which the bench need no longer warn themselves of the danger of convicting on the uncorroborated evidence of a child. The bench must always consider the dangers of hysterical invention or exaggeration, and the possibility of collusion between child witnesses. These dangers should always be stressed to the bench during a closing speech. If the bench is in doubt, corroboration should be sought, regardless of the age of the child: *R* v *Morgan* [14]. Nonetheless, the sworn evidence of one child is capable of corroborating that of another, or, as pointed out above, the unsworn evidence of another.

(b) Accomplices. An accomplice is a witness who is himself either a participant in the offence charged, or in offences of which evidence is admitted under the similar-fact rule, or who, in a trial for theft, is a handler by receiving of the goods alleged to have been stolen. Not infrequently, accomplices have pleaded guilty and give their evidence in expectation of or in gratitude for a lenient sentence. Their motives are almost always suspect, and so, accordingly, is their evidence. In some cases, the witness is exposed as an accomplice only during the course of his evidence. In *Davies* v *DPP* [15], the House of Lords held that the categories of accomplice described above were the only ones known to the law. But whether a witness is in any given circumstances an accomplice, as thus defined, is a question of fact on which you should address the court, if appropriate.

(c) Complainants of sexual misconduct. In some ways, the evidence of these witnesses is equated with that of children, because of the possibility of invention, exaggeration or collusion. Where, as not infrequently happens, the complainant is also a child, the danger is proportionately greater and the bench must take extreme care to warn themselves of the dangers of uncorroborated evidence.

In summary trial, corroboration has assumed a less important role than in jury trial. The reason for this is simply that in jury trial, it is possible to discern from the summing-up whether the judge adequately directs the jury not to convict in the absence of corroboration, or warns them of the danger of convicting on uncorroborated evidence, as the case may be. In summary trial, the magistrates do not audibly direct or warn themselves. This does not mean that the rules governing corroboration are unimportant in summary trial, though they are regrettably often overlooked. A defence advocate should request the magistrates to seek advice from their clerk on the legal aspects of corroboration, and should invite the clerk to advise the bench whether there is any evidence capable of constituting corroboration. If appropriate, the advocate should invite the clerk to advise the bench that the absence of corroboration must be fatal to a conviction. In any event, the danger of uncorroborated evidence always makes first-class material for a closing speech, and should always be stressed.

What kinds of witnesses should I call to give evidence?

At first, this may appear to be a somewhat strange question. It is intended, not to refer to the personal characteristics of a witness, or even to draw attention to the fact that there are good and bad witnesses, but to point out that some species of witness are often overlooked and excluded from consideration. It is deceptively easy to get into the habit of thinking that witnesses must necessarily be percipient witnesses, that is to say witnesses who perceived relevant facts and who are called to give direct evidence of what they perceived. This way of thinking omits reference to two valuable and underused species of witness, namely the expert witness and the character witness.

Expert witnesses   As long ago as 1782, Lord Mansfield said in *Folkes* v *Chadd* [16] that the opinion of scientific men, upon proven facts, might be given by men of science within their own science. It was a recognition of the plain truth that courts may be equipped to decide questions within the common experience of judges, jurors and magistrates, but are not equipped to deal with technical matters calling for specialised expertise. Experts are therefore permitted to state their opinion on such matters, on the basis of proven, admitted or even hypothetical facts, in order to assist the court in reaching a conclusion which it would be incapable of reaching properly unaided.

An expert is somebody who, in the context of the specialised area facing the court, knows what he or she is talking about and is therefore capable of rendering to the court the necessary advice. There are provisions for courts to obtain expert assistance, independently of the parties, but in most cases, expert witnesses are called by the parties. It is often, though erroneously, assumed that experts are an expensive luxury inappropriate to the magistrates' or the county court. Such is not the case. Since the only qualification to be an expert is to know what you are talking about, experts may be recruited in back-street garages as well as engineering departments of universities. Qualification by long experience is almost always just as persuasive as qualification on paper, and frequently more so. Experts qualified by experience are often inexpensive, often enthusiastic and often decisive. The court is concerned with actual expertise, and not with the means by which that expertise has been obtained. In *R* v *Silverlock* [17], a solicitor who had made a study of handwriting was permitted to give evidence as an expert in that field, notwithstanding his lack of formal qualification. Stories abound of cases won by witnesses with a lifetime's experience of nuts and bolts, over 'highly qualified' theoretical engineers.

It is certainly true that qualification in the relevant field is necessary. It is, in fact, a question of competence to give evidence, since with very limited exceptions, only experts are permitted to state their opinion rather than to give evidence of facts. You must, therefore, present evidence of the qualifications of the witness to the court and specifically invite the court to accept the witness as an expert, before leading the witness on to deal with substantive matters. This, however, is easily accomplished by asking the witness about paper qualifications or experience in the field, or preferably both. The modern practice is to permit a witness to testify as an expert, if he or she has any serious claim to do so. The weight of an expert's evidence is quite another matter, and depends on how far the expert can persuade the court that his or her opinion can be treated as reliable.

For these very reasons, you are entitled to cross-examine a witness tendered as an expert, before he or she testifies about any substantive matter, concerning the question of qualification, with a view to suggesting that the witness is not qualified to be an expert, and that the proposed evidence is therefore inadmissible from the witness tendered. This cross-examination should take place after the credentials of the witness have been presented in chief, and before substantive opinion evidence is given. It is proper and sometimes necessary to interrupt the evidence in chief at the right moment, and ask the court for leave to cross-examine, which should not be refused, since the cross-examination is relevant to competence as a witness and must be conducted at that stage. While the court will usually decide to hear the witness, such cross-examination is never wasted. It plants in the mind of the court some doubt as to the weight of the evidence to come, and enables you to begin your attack on the other side's expert evidence even before it is given.

In the next chapter, we shall consider expert evidence in more detail, dealing with the handling of expert witnesses and with the important rules of court calling for disclosure of expert reports in civil cases.

Character witnesses The evidence which may be given by character witnesses has been dealt with in Chapter 5. However, it is well worth noting again that such witnesses are a proper and sadly underused weapon available to an advocate representing a defendant of good or reformed character. The witness must, of course, know the defendant well enough to speak with some authority, and must himself be demonstrably credible and respectable. Always ask your client if such a person is available to speak for him. Ensure, of course, that your witness is familiar with the defendant's character including any previous convictions, especially if the defendant is a reformed character. Few things are worse than having your character witness learn for the first time in cross-examination that the defendant's record is not quite as unblemished as he believed and came to court to say.

Notes

1. [1917] 1 KB 283.
2. (1924) 18 Cr App R 100.
3. [1944] 2 All ER 311.
4. (1632) 3 St Tr 402.
5. [1963] 1 QB 285.
6. [1974] 1 WLR 894.
7. [1954] 1 QB 279.
8. [1977] 1 WLR 234.
9. [1979] AC 474.
10. The privilege was abolished except in relation to criminal proceedings by the Civil Evidence Act 1968, s. 16(3).
11. (1946) 31 Cr App R 146.
12. [1960] 1 WLR 1239.
13. [1973] AC 296.
14. [1978] 1 WLR 735.
15. [1954] AC 378.
16. (1782) 3 Doug KB 157.
17. [1894] 2 QB 766.

Seven

Expert Evidence

Introduction

Witnesses are called in a court of law to state the facts which they have observed and they are not allowed to give their opinion to the court on those facts. So, for example, a witness can say that a car was being driven on the wrong side of the road or at a speed of 60 miles per hour, but strictly speaking he is not allowed to say that in his opinion the driving that he saw was dangerous. Although often nobody bothers to take the point when a witness oversteps the mark and ventures his opinion it is still a basic rule of law that witnesses are not in court to give their views about the matters in issue. There is, however, a very important exception to this rule and that relates to the evidence of expert witnesses. A person who has acquired expertise in a specialised field either by learning and studying or by experience (or both) is entitled to state his opinion to the court because he has a knowledge and understanding of the specialised matters in question which the judge or magistrates cannot possibly hope to have. Therefore the court will allow him to give to them an 'informed opinion'.

Expert witnesses are not often called to give evidence orally in cases in magistrates' courts; instead their evidence is given usually in the form of witness statements which are not challenged (for example, fingerprint evidence or the evidence of blood/alcohol analysis). In county court actions, on the other hand, expert evidence is very frequently presented orally and is often challenged; indeed, in many cases, the principal area of dispute will lie in the conflicting opinions of expert witnesses. For example, the court may have to resolve differences between the opinions given by architects called to give evidence about what went wrong with a building or the court may have to decide between two expert engineers who have each attempted to explain why a motor-car engine has broken down. Because expert opinion is so important in county court actions the lawyer needs a very good understanding of the rules relating to such evidence and the techniques whereby it can be tested.

Preparation of expert evidence

When you have to consider your own expert's opinion you will be faced immediately with a problem which will never arise when you are dealing with the proofs of the other witnesses you are going to call. Those witnesses will speak about the facts — what was said before the contract was made, what manoeuvres were executed by the vehicles prior to the collision taking place — and you can apply your own common sense and knowledge in determining the value which is to be placed upon the accounts given by the different witnesses. In the same way, you will be able to rely upon your own experience of people and events to decide on the line of cross-examination you should take in dealing with the witnesses of fact called on the other side.

The position is altogether different when you are considering expert testimony. You are called upon to understand and decide the value of evidence on a subject of which you will have, at best, only a rudimentary knowledge; and you will be required to undertake the very difficult task of challenging evidence given on the other side by a person with years of experience in the field in question. This is obviously a formidable task.

The key to dealing successfully with expert evidence is *preparation*. The preparation starts when you first have the report of your own expert to hand. Whatever the subject-matter, whether it is a medical report, a surveyor's report, an engineer's report, whatever it may be, you must begin by making a very serious effort to understand your own expert's evidence. You should build up a library of useful reference books — a medical dictionary, a simple guide to house building and repairs, a book with good diagrams showing the workings of a motor car — such reference books (the simpler the better) can be indispensable.

Once you as the advocate have had a chance to form some idea of the points your expert is making in his report you may well feel that you need to see him in conference. If he is going to be called as a witness at the trial, you will not get very far unless you have had a chance to go over in detail with him the report which he has made.

When you see your expert in conference do not worry about

knowing less of the subject than the expert does. No lawyer likes to confess ignorance (particularly not in front of a client) but the advocate cannot afford to pretend to an expert witness an understanding that he or she does not possess. The only sensible technique is to start off by telling the expert quite frankly that you have no knowledge of this particular field — and neither will the judge who at the end of the day will have to decide the case. Your expert must therefore be prepared to teach you just so much of the subject as is necessary for you to understand the points that will be made in evidence. If you do not understand the explanation, make the expert go back over it again. Ask the expert to draw simple diagrams to explain to you the points that will be covered. This can be time consuming but in doing it you will not only be teaching yourself the essential matters you have to understand before you can conduct your case, you will also be working out how the expert's evidence can be presented in the most attractive and readily understood way when you arrive at court.

At some stage, assuming the case is going to be contested, you should receive copies of the expert evidence which your opponent proposes to adduce. The rules of court relating to this will be dealt with later, but it may be assumed as a basic principle that you are never going to allow the other side to put you in the position where you have to go into court in a contested case without seeing in advance the expert evidence against you. What do you do when you have obtained the report from the other side?

You are going to need the assistance of your own expert again. You could not possibly cross-examine the expert on the other side until you have had the advice of your own expert on this new report. So you must persuade your expert first to explain to you what is being said in the other side's report; then, ask for an explanation of why (if it be the case) your expert says the other expert is wrong. He may be wrong for a number of reasons: he may be acting on a version of the facts which you can prove is untrue; he may have omitted to notice some important point picked up by your expert; his opinion may be based on knowledge which is outdated. But, before you can even attempt to cross-examine, you will need to understand why it is that your expert has come to a different conclusion from the expert on the other side.

Be careful not to be overwhelmed by your own expert. It can be very easy to give up when an expert has lost you midway through an explanation of some technical matter. You must not do this because the chances are that if the expert has lost you, in due course, he will lose the judge too. Lastly, be prepared for the possibility that your expert is wrong; if he is wrong, it is best to discover this before costs are expended on a full-scale trial of the action; bear in mind that you are under a duty to your client to make sure that the expert evidence you have obtained will stand up in court.

In practice, expert evidence is usually exchanged well before the trial. Our court system is only able to cope with the volume of work which it has because most cases are settled before trial; often an important consideration in determining whether or not to advise your client to settle an action is the view which you as an advocate have formed upon the strength of the expert evidence. Sometimes, of course, it will be clear from the moment you read your own report that your case simply cannot proceed; more often it will not be until after an overall picture can be built up, by looking at the documentation revealed on discovery and the views of the experts on both sides, that you will be able to form a good idea of whether or not you are going to win at the end of the day, and whether or not you should settle and if so on what terms.

Therefore, both from the point of view of preparing your own case and as a means of deciding whether or not you should settle, you will need to see the other side's expert evidence. The next part of this chapter considers the law and the rules of court on this topic.

Disclosure of expert evidence before trial

The basic rule at common law is that you are *not* entitled to know your opponent's expert evidence before the trial takes place unless he is willing to disclose it to you. The reason for this is that expert evidence is covered by legal professional privilege [1]. Letters, conversations, any communications between a lay person and his solicitor for the purpose of obtaining legal advice are privileged: they cannot be revealed without the client's consent. In the same way, a proof of evidence or a letter from a witness to a solicitor is covered by professional privilege and for the purpose of such privilege it makes no difference whether that proof of evidence or letter comes from a lay witness or an expert witness. The rule of the law of evidence which underlies the whole practice concerning the exchange of experts' reports is this: you are entitled to refuse disclosure of expert evidence because it is privileged. This means that if you obtain an expert report which does not say what you were hoping to hear, then you are completely free to discard that opinion and try another expert to see if you can do better. There is no duty on you to disclose evidence which you do not propose to use in court.

On the other hand, when you have obtained a report which you decide to use at trial, then a different set of rules applies. The Civil Evidence Act 1972 expressly provides that the rule concerning privilege is not to be used as a way of concealing expert evidence until the trial; the Act provides for rules of court to be made to require each side to give notice to the other of the expert evidence they intend to call at the trial. CCR, Ord. 20, r.27, requires that (unless all the parties agree or the judge gives special permission) no expert evidence can be given at the trial unless the party wishing to call that evidence has applied in advance to the registrar to determine whether there should be disclosure of the evidence and has complied with any order that the registrar has made.

This means that by the time of the pre-trial review you should have made up your mind whether you are going to need expert evidence, and should have obtained that evidence and be in a position to decide whether or not you want to argue that there should not be disclosure.

The registrar is directed by CCR, Ord. 20, r.28, to apply the High Court rules. RSC, Ord. 38, r.37, provides that in personal injury cases the court *shall* order each party to disclose in advance the expert evidence they are going to adduce at the hearing. The only exceptions to this are where the reports deal with questions of medical negligence or there is an issue concerning the genuineness of the plaintiff's symptoms or whether the injuries in question were caused by the accident; in those three cases the court may decide that there should not be disclosure.

RSC, Ord. 38, r.38, deals with expert evidence in other cases and the wording of the order gives the court a discretion whether or not to order disclosure. In practice, the courts have taken the view that disclosure should always be ordered unless there are very good reasons to the contrary [2]. The sort of exceptional case where disclosure will not be ordered is where the expert has been given one party's proofs of evidence and asked to comment on the assumption that they are correct; to order disclosure in such a case would in effect be to order one side to reveal in advance the contents of their proofs of evidence to the other side [3].

It is likely that at the pre-trial review the registrar will order *mutual* disclosure of expert evidence. By that, he means you are bound to disclose your expert evidence to the other side when they tell you that they are ready to disclose their reports. This does not mean that you have to produce the reports of experts you have decided not to call; nor does it mean that you have to show the other side every letter from your own expert or every attendance note that you may have made; what you are required to do is to give the other side a written report fairly setting out the evidence which your expert will give at trial.

Of course, it is one thing to have an order in your favour and it is another thing to see that your opponent complies with that order. What should you do if you have your report ready and are willing to exchange it but your opponent says he has not yet obtained a report? Sometimes the best advice is not to disclose; if you do disclose your report you may find that your opponent will then take it to an expert who will proceed to tear your expert's opinion into shreds. If you feel that this could happen, do not disclose your report but go back to the registrar and ask him to make an 'unless order', i.e., an order that unless the other side produce a report and disclose it within so many days they shall be debarred from calling expert evidence. This technique is a sensible one to employ in High Court litigation and in a substantial claim in the county court. However, there will be other cases where you may decide that it would be sensible to reveal your report even though the other side have not yet obtained a report themselves; it may be that on seeing your report the other side will give up and put forward sensible terms of compromise. This matter obviously requires careful judgment. What you should never allow is a situation in which you are going into court to face expert evidence which has not been disclosed to you.

Presentation of expert evidence at trial

How do you deal with your own expert when you arrive at court? First, of course, have the original copy of his report ready for the judge and ask the judge to read this immediately before your expert is called to give evidence. Then, remembering the things you did not understand when you first read the report, ask your expert to go over those points.

You must work out an acceptable formula to conceal from the judge the fact that you are concerned he may not have understood some of the points in the report. Every advocate has to determine such a formula for himself; but what is important is that you should make sure that all the points which are in any way obscure are cleared up before your expert is tendered for cross-examination. Bear in mind that, unlike other witnesses, an expert may not only state his opinion, but many explain and justify that opinion by reference to the exhibits, results of tests, analyses or experiments, or authoritative published works.

When you come to cross-examine you should have in front of you a list of questions prepared by your expert and you should understand the point of each of those questions. Expert witnesses usually charge considerable fees and you are entitled to insist that they remain in court for all the relevant evidence including the evidence of the expert on the other side. It may well be that in hearing the evidence of the lay witnesses your expert will decide that he has to qualify or change his opinion. It may also be that in hearing the testimony given by the expert on the other side he will want to alter or re-emphasise certain points in his own evidence. You are entitled to expect your expert to be on hand throughout all those parts of the trial where his presence would be helpful. It is normally a false economy to call the expert for half an hour and then let him depart.

Summary

To sum up the points in this chapter, there are three essential points which you need to remember if you are to succeed in putting forward expert evidence. First, preparation — you must be willing to spend three or even four times as long in preparing expert evidence as you would in proofing witnesses who are merely speaking about the facts. Secondly, candour — you must be frank with your expert so that he understands your own ignorance of the subject and explains it to you with such clarity that before you go into court you fully understand the points that he is making; if you do not understand the evidence he is going to give, there is little chance that you will be able to present your case properly. Lastly, a knowledge of the rules — the advocate must know what the rules say and be able to use them to his client's advantage; in the field of expert evidence this means that the advocate must be able to use the rules so as to prevent himself from being taken in any way by surprise.

Notes

1. *Causton* v *Mann Egerton (Johnsons) Ltd* [1974] 1 WLR 162.
2. *Ollett* v *Bristol Aerojet Ltd* [1979] 1 WLR 1197 (practice note).
3. *Rahman* v *Kirklees Area Health Authority* [1980] 3 All ER 610.

Eight

Presentation of Evidence at Trial

Introduction

This chapter is concerned with the rules of evidence relating to the examination of witnesses and the introduction of evidence at trial. Every witness called is subject to examination by the party calling him, all other parties and the court. The advocate must, therefore, be familiar with the rules governing examination-in-chief, cross-examination, re-examination and examination by the court.

In civil cases, the parties and any witnesses may remain in court throughout the trial, unless otherwise ordered by the judge on the application of any party [1]. Unless there is a serious basis for suspecting that evidence on the other side may be dishonest, it is generally best not to invite the judge to exclude witnesses, since your own witnesses will also be excluded. In criminal cases, on the other hand, with the exception of the defendant and any expert witnesses, any witness waiting to give evidence must remain outside court until called. A bench will almost certainly attach less weight to the evidence of a witness who has been in court listening to the evidence before being called, because of the possibility that his evidence has been tailored to what he has heard. After giving evidence, witnesses must remain in court for the duration of the trial, unless released by the court. Unless there is a substantial likelihood that the witness may be recalled, it is proper and kind to ask that he be released.

Examination-in-chief is the process whereby a party calling a witness seeks to elicit from that witness facts favourable to his case. Examination-in-chief must be conducted without leading questions, and subject to a number of important rules of evidence, which will be considered shortly.

Any witness called is liable to be cross-examined by each other party. In a criminal trial, the witness is cross-examined by the defendants in the order in which they are named in the charge or charges, and lastly, in the case of a defendant or defence witness, by the prosecution.

Cross-examination has two purposes, the first being to challenge the witness's evidence in chief, in all respects in which it does not correspond with the cross-examiner's instructions, and the second being to elicit or further emphasise facts favourable to the cross-examiner which were either not referred to or insufficiently emphasised in chief. The second purpose suggests, correctly, that a witness is liable to cross-examination once called, even if he has given no evidence in chief, as witness the convenient practice of simply tendering corroborative police officers for cross-examination. Questions may be asked in cross-examination, not only to challenge the substance of the evidence in chief directly, but also to attack the credit of the witness by showing that he is lying, exaggerating, had insufficient opportunity to observe the events about which he is giving evidence, or that his recollection is unsatisfactory. Except in the case of a defendant giving evidence, a witness may also be discredited directly by cross-examination about his previous bad character.

Re-examination, a much neglected art, is the process whereby a party who has called a witness may seek to explain or clarify any evidence given during cross-examination, which appears to be damaging or unfavourable on the facts or in terms of the witness's credit. Questions in re-examination must be confined to matters raised during cross-examination. But the cross-examiner should be aware that, if a matter is raised during cross-examination, it may be fully explored in re-examination. The cross-examination will have opened the subject up for exploration, even if the evidence would have been inadmissible had the re-examiner tried to introduce it in chief.

The judge or bench (acting through the chairman or clerk) may put questions to a witness, in order to clarify any matter which is unclear to them. Courts vary a great deal in the number of questions they ask. Some will even interrupt an advocate to ask them. Disconcerting as this may be, it is inadvisable to object, unless the witness is your client and the interruptions are making examination of him practically impossible to conduct, or the questions seem to be having the effect of harrassing, intimidating or upsetting your client. This is relatively unusual, but where it occurs, you must explain to the court the difficulties which the interruptions are causing for you or your client, and politely suggest that the court defer its questions until the end of your client's evidence. It is proper and advisable to ask leave to put further questions arising from any answers given in response to the court.

We now proceed to examine in more detail a number of important rules of evidence concerning examination-in-chief, cross-examination and re-examination.

Examination-in-chief

Leading questions The use of leading questions is improper in examination-in-chief and in re-examination, and evidence elicited by means of leading questions, while not inadmissible, is of very slight weight [2]. This basic rule is easy to state, but far from easy to apply. The story is told of counsel who, when representing a client charged with larceny (it is quite an old story) of a pig, placed his client in the witness-box, and asked him: 'Mr D, is it right that you were walking down the road, when you found the pig, the subject of this indictment?' Counsel for the prosecution was ungracious enough to object to this as a leading question, and the judge ordered it to be rephrased. After some thought, counsel asked his client: 'Mr D, by what means were you proceeding down the road, when you found the pig?'

Up to a point, all the characters involved in the story were correct. Counsel for the prosecution was correct in his objection that the question was leading, and the judge was correct to rule that it must be rephrased. Counsel for the defendant correctly identified one of the two areas in which his question was leading. His rephrasing was partially successful, in that it offered the witness a free hand to describe his method of progress along the road. This, however, did nothing to legitimate the form of the question, in so far as it related to the far more important issue of how the defendant had come by the pig. In this respect, the question was not improved at all.

What was counsel's error in posing these questions? It was that they tended to put words into the witness's mouth, or to suggest directly to the witness the evidence that counsel expected to receive. To present evidence by means of a series of leading questions is to do no more than use the vocal chords of the witness to make a prepared speech to the court, whereas the court is concerned to hear the evidence in the words of the witness, not of the advocate. In the example given, the witness was being invited merely to assent to counsel's statement of how he came by the pig.

It is not easy to avoid leading questions, and experience, including time spent listening to how other advocates bring out evidence without them, is the best teacher. As a general guide, the 'two-for-one rule' is useful. This rule draws attention to the fact that leading questions are defective primarily because they are too specifically worded. To avoid this, ask two questions instead of one, to get at the same fact. The first question takes a step back from the desired result, and will be phrased in general terms. You will ask whether something happened, whether the witness went somewhere, or the like, inviting a yes-or-no answer. Having got the answer to that, your second question will invite the specific detail implied in the answer to the first question, but still without actually putting the answer into the witness's mouth. Using the two-for-one rule, let us see how counsel should have elicited the fact that his client's possession of the pig was innocent. The examination-in-chief might proceed as follows:

Q   Mr D, did there come a time on the day in question when you went out?

A   Yes.

Q   Where did you go?

A   I walked down Lover's Lane.

Q   While you were in Lover's Lane, did anything come to your attention?

A   Yes.

Q   What was that?

A   I saw a pig coming towards me in the middle of the road.

Q   As a result of seeing the pig, did you do anything?

A   Yes.

Q   What did you do?

A   I got hold of the pig and began to walk along the road with it, so that I could return it to a field.

Q   At that time, was any other person on the scene?

A   Not at that time. But a minute or so later, a policeman came and accused me of stealing the pig.

Notice that counsel has asked two questions rather than one, to establish where the defendant went, what he did, and how he came by the pig. The court has now heard the evidence in the language of the witness, yet counsel retained control throughout by leaving the witness in no doubt of the answer which should be given. This is the essence of good examination-in-chief.

For reasons of practical convenience, leading questions in chief are permitted in the following limited circumstances, because there can be no objection to them:

(a) On purely preliminary matters not directly related to the facts in issue. Usually, but not invariably, such matters as the witness's name, address and occupation would fall under this head.

(b) On any matters not in dispute.

(c) Where a witness is going to deal with a fact which has already been established by other evidence, he may be asked directly about that fact.

(d) In any case where all advocates in the case agree that leading questions shall be permitted in certain areas. This is a helpful practice, which saves time and facilitates the examination-in-chief, though care must be taken to define the areas in which leading is to be permitted, and you should not hesitate to object if leading questions are asked on other subjects not covered by the agreement.

(e) Where leave has been granted to treat a witness as hostile, in which case the examination-in-chief partakes of the nature of cross-examination. This topic is dealt with later in this chapter.

Memory-refreshing documents. In criminal cases, it is a common sight to see a police officer, who has just been sworn, reach into his pocket and produce a notebook, to which he asks to refer, in order to refresh his memory while giving evidence. Almost always, the court agrees, and the officer refers to, or even reads from, the notebook while giving evidence. This is a perfectly proper procedure, but not because it is a criminal case, or because the witness happens to be a police officer, or because the document happens to be a notebook.

In civil and criminal cases alike, any witness may, with leave to the court, refresh his memory while giving evidence, by reference to any document which was made or verified by the witness, contemporaneously with the events to which it relates. It is important to note that the requirements of contemporaneous making or verification, which will be examined below, apply only where the reference is made in the witness-box and while giving evidence. A witness may look at any material outside court, for the purpose of refreshing his memory [3], and it is usually good practice to show your witness a copy of his proof of evidence or statement before he goes into court, so that the giving of evidence is not reduced to a test of memory. Even though the witness would not be permitted to refer to such non-contemporaneous documents while in the witness-box, there is absolutely no objection to his doing so before giving evidence.

Once the witness steps into the box, the rules come into play. The first rule is that the document must have been made or verified by the witness. The best type of document is one, which, like the police officer's notebook, was made for the express purpose of later reference. But this is not a requirement. Literally any document, however made, will suffice, for example, the cigarette packet on which the witness scrawled the number of the car. The witness need not even have made the document personally, provided that he verified it, that is to say that he either saw it being made, or read it soon enough after another had made it to be 'contemporaneous', and in either case, that he checked its contents at that time and acknowledged them to be accurate. Hence the practice whereby a police officer makes a note reflecting the joint recollection of himself and his colleague, while the colleague verifies the note, and both thereafter refer to it while giving evidence.

The second rule is that the making or verification of the document must have been 'contemporaneous' with the events to which the document refers. The word 'contemporaneous' cannot, of course, be construed literally. Although a literally contemporaneous note can sometimes be made, for example, where a record is made of an interview as it proceeds, many events leave no leisure for the making of notes as they actually occur. The rule is, therefore, that the note must have been made at the first practicable opportunity, and while the events were fresh in the mind of the witness. This is a matter of fact and degree in every case, and there is no set time, beyond which a document is no longer contemporaneous. The purpose of the requirement is to confine reference to presumptively accurate records, and any unexplained delay in making a note is to be regarded with some suspicion. In very exceptional cases, even two weeks has been held to be 'contemporaneous', but in the absence of a good explanation for the delay, even a few hours may be fatal.

Although in many cases, defence advocates allow the officer's request to go unchallenged, it is a matter for the court to be satisfied that a reference in the witness-box is proper. A prosecutor should in every case ask preliminary questions of the witness to establish whether the document falls within the rules, and these should not be put in the leading form all too often heard, such as 'Were the events fresh in your mind when you made the note?' A defence advocate can and should object both to a failure to lay a foundation for the note, and to any attempt to lead in the foundational questions. The defence may cross-examine the witness, solely on the issue of whether reference to the document is proper, before any evidence in chief is given. Although in almost every case, the witness will be allowed to refresh his memory — rightly so, since the giving of evidence should be a test of honesty and accuracy, rather than of memory — your cross-examination is far from pointless. You will, if you wish, get an early look at the document. And if the contemporaneity of the document is marginal, you will have cast doubt on the witness's evidence before it is even given. This doubt will increase if it transpires that the witness has no or little independent recollection of the events, and is relying entirely or substantially on the document. You will then start your main cross-examination at quite an advantage.

It not infrequently happens that a police officer's notebook, or other contemporaneous document is lost before trial. If, before the notebook is lost, the officer has made a copy of the note, or has compiled a statement by copying the note out, there is no reason why he should not refresh his memory from what he has copied, since the original was made contemporaneously: *R v Cheng* [4]. And in *Attorney-General's Reference (No. 3 of 1979)* [5], it was held proper for an officer to refresh his memory from a note compiled partly from a literally contemporaneous rough note of an interview, and partly from his own recollection, even though the finished note was not identical to the rough note.

A memory-refreshing document is not evidence of the truth of the facts recorded in it, because it is hearsay and inadmissible for that purpose. By referring to the document, the witness does not make it evidence. The evidence is what the witness states from the witness-box, not what is contained in the document. Although this may seem an academic distinction, especially where the witness apparently has no independent recollection and reads word for word from the document, it has important consequences in cross-examination.

Cross-examination using memory-refreshing documents will be dealt with later in this chapter.

Previous consistent statements   A witness may not seek to enhance his evidence by relating to the court what he himself has said on the same subject on another occasion. Such statements, known as previous consistent or self-serving statements, are in reality a form of hearsay, and do not add anything of value to the evidence of the witness. They are inadmissible at common law, which applies to criminal trials in the magistrates' court. In *R* v *Roberts* [6], the defendant was charged with murder. His defence was that the killing had been accidental. It was held that the defendant was not entitled to state in evidence that, two days after the killing, he had told his father that it had been an accident.

In civil cases, in keeping with the different, statutory rules governing hearsay, there would seem to be no reason why previous consistent statements should not be admissible as evidence of the facts stated by virtue of s. 2(1) of the Civil Evidence Act 1968, although the weight of such statements would generally be slight.

In certain exceptional cases, previous consistent statements are admissible even at common law. These cases are as follows:

(a)   In a few unusual cases, a witness may relate to the court an excited utterance or spontaneous exclamation which he (or another) made in the excitement of the event which he is describing in evidence. This is a common-law exception to the hearsay rule, which applies to previous consistent statements, and is dealt with in detail in Chapter 2. It applies only where the utterance is so closely related in time and circumstances to the event itself as to be part of that event, and where the court can be satisfied that the utterance was not calculated by the witness for his own advantage. In other words, the statement must not have been deliberately self-serving.

(b)   Where a witness has identified the defendant as the perpetrator of the offence charged, the witness may state that he previously made an out-of-court identification of the defendant. Although such a statement is self-serving, assuming that the witness maintains in evidence that the defendant was the perpetrator, it is in the interests of the defendant, no less than of the prosecution, that a witness should be given the chance to identify a suspect at an early stage, preferably on an identification parade, and the results of such identification are held to be admissible for reasons of obvious practicality.

(c) Where the charge is one of a sexual offence, the complainant may give evidence that he or she made a 'recent complaint' about the offence. This complaint must have been made at the first reasonably practicable opportunity, so that there is a reasonable inference that it is not deliberately self-serving. The evidence of the complaint may include any statement of the identity of the offender. The evidence of the complaint has a strictly limited value, and is admissible only to confirm the complainant's evidence (in so far as consistent) or to rebut or disprove consent on the part of the complainant, if consent is an issue in the case. The complaint is not evidence of the truth of the matters complained of, and cannot offer corroboration of the evidence of the complainant at trial.

(d) Where a witness is cross-examined in such a way as to suggest that he has, within a specific period of time, fabricated his evidence, the witness may rebut this suggestion by relating that he made a statement consistent with his evidence at a time prior to the alleged fabrication. This is known as rebutting an allegation of recent fabrication, and although it arises generally in re-examination rather than examination-in-chief, may properly be dealt with here.

The right does not arise merely because it is suggested to the witness that he is not telling the truth. There must be a suggestion, made expressly or by necessary implication, that there was a fabrication of evidence at or after some time, so that the timing of the prior statement has evidential value in rebutting the suggestion. In *R* v *Oyesiku* [7], the defendant's wife gave evidence on his behalf. It was suggested to her in cross-examination that she had prepared her evidence in collusion with her husband. In rebuttal of this suggestion, it was admissible for the wife to give evidence that, after the defendant's arrest and before she had had any opportunity to speak with him, she had made a statement to the defendant's solicitor consistent with her evidence in chief. A previous consistent statement tendered to rebut a suggestion of recent fabrication in a criminal trial in the magistrates' court is, by virtue of common law, admissible only to rebut the suggestion, and is not evidence of the facts contained in the statement. In civil cases, such a statement is also admissible as evidence of the facts stated by virtue of s. 3(1)(b) of the Civil Evidence Act 1968, although its weight for this purpose may not be great.

Unfavourable and hostile witnesses   Witnesses who fail to come up to proof, who in other words prove to be unfavourable, or less favourable in their evidence than might have been anticipated, are one of the hazards of litigation. Whatever care has been taken in interviewing witnesses and in preparing proofs of evidence, it is inevitable that occasionally some disastrous departure from the anticipated evidence will occur. There is sometimes a lesson to be learned here, namely never to call a witness merely because the witness is available. However much your client may believe in the witness, offer to produce the witness at court and try to pressure you into calling the witness, you should always rely in the end on your professional judgment of the witness and of the anticipated evidence. Avoid calling a witness from whom you do not have a signed proof of evidence, unless it appears really necessary. However, the disaster of the witness who fails to come up to proof is not necessarily a question of failure to learn these lessons, but can strike the most careful advocate in almost any situation, and without warning. What can be done to salvage the case?

As in many situations in advocacy, the most effective solution is the simplest, and is often overlooked. This is to call any other evidence at your disposal, having got the witness out of the witness-box as quickly as possible. It may be that the remaining evidence will be sufficient to win the case. The fact that you have had the misfortune to call an unfavourable witness is not always fatal, especially if the points of inconsistency are not of the most material kind, and other witnesses may be able to convince the court to disregard the unfavourable parts of the evidence. Remember, however, to be ruthlessly honest and realistic in your closing speech. Face, and do not try to fudge the fact that there is evidence against you which you yourself have called. The court will know this anyway, and to try to conceal it is a dreadful error of judgment. Face the problem and then work to overcome it by stressing the other available evidence.

In some cases, of course, you will have no other evidence, or the effect of the unfavourable evidence will be irreparable. In such a case, you may wish to impeach, or in other words directly discredit your own witness. This you can only do if the court adjudges the witness to be hostile, instead of merely unfavourable. It is obviously embarrassing and undesirable that a party should be permitted to impeach a witness whom he has tendered to the court as a witness of truth. However, where the witness is hostile, this is allowed in order to protect a party against deliberate sabotage of his case. A hostile witness, for this purpose, is one who displays an inimical animus towards the party calling him or evinces no desire to give evidence fairly or to tell the truth. Hostility may stem from malice, bribery, intimidation or from a mere indisposition to cooperate. In dealing with such a witness, you can pray in aid s. 3 of the Criminal Procedure Act 1865, which provides rather inelegantly that:

> A party producing a witness shall not be allowed to impeach his credit by general evidence of bad character; but he may, in case the witness shall in the opinion of the judge prove adverse, contradict him by other evidence, or, by leave of the judge, prove that he has made at other times a statement inconsistent with his present testimony; but before such last-mentioned proof can be given the circumstances of the supposed statement, sufficient to designate the particular occasion, must be mentioned to the witness, and he must be asked whether or not he has made such statement.

The section applies, despite the name of the statute, to civil and criminal cases alike. It provides two weapons for use against the 'adverse' (which has been interpreted judicially to mean 'hostile') witness. Both require leave of the court, which must be applied for in every case, by submitting to the court frankly that the witness is hostile and not just unfavourable. This involves jettisoning the witness, and therefore requires a crucial exercise of judgment on how bad the damage is, the likelihood that your case may be totally sabotaged if you do nothing, and whether or not you can prove your case without the witness. In the case of the prosecution, it is the duty of the prosecutor to show to the bench the statement of any witness who proves to be hostile, and to ask leave to treat the witness as such [8].

Having obtained leave, you may either call evidence to discredit the witness directly (contradicting the witness rather than merely proving your case by other evidence) or cross-examine the witness about any previous statement (such as his witness statement, deposition, evidence in former proceedings or proof of evidence) which is inconsistent with his present evidence. Note that what you are doing is designed to discredit the witness, not prove facts. At common law, and therefore in criminal trials in the magistrates' court, evidence of such a prior inconsistent statement is evidence only of the inconsistency of the witness, and is not evidence of the facts contained in the previous statement. In civil cases, s. 3(1) of the Civil Evidence Act 1968 permits previous inconsistent statements to be used for either or both purposes, but their weight as evidence of the facts previously stated is generally only substantial where it can be shown that the previous statement was made prior to the time when the malice, bribery or intimidation of the witness commenced, and is therefore apparently reliable.

Note also the procedural requirements of the section, in terms of identifying the previous statement to the witness and asking him to admit that he made it. There is nothing in the section which prevents reference to a previous verbal statement, but if the witness denies making it, there is not much you can do except call someone who heard it, and hope for the best. It will not be very convincing. This amply illustrates the rule that signed proofs should be obtained whenever possible.

In *R* v *Thompson* [9], the victim of an alleged offence of incest was called for the prosecution, but refused to give evidence. The trial judge permitted her to be treated as hostile. It was argued on appeal that this was improper, because the witness having given no evidence, there was no 'present testimony', with which the previous statement could be said to be inconsistent. While accepting that this was a sound argument in terms of s. 3 of the 1865 Act, the Court of Appeal held that the trial court retained power at common law to satisfy the ends of justice by treating a silent, uncooperative witness in the same way as a vocal one.

Cross-examination

Cross-examination has two purposes: to challenge the evidence in chief in so far as it conflicts with your instructions; and to elicit facts favourable to your case which have not emerged, or which were insufficiently emphasised in chief. In Chapter 10, we shall see how these objectives should be borne in mind when preparing a cross-examination. This chapter will examine the rules of evidence which underlie the conduct of cross-examination.

The main evidential reason for cross-examining any witness is that a failure to cross-examine may be taken by the court as an acceptance of any part of the examination-in-chief which is not challenged: *R* v *Bircham* [10]. This means that the cross-examiner should cross-examine the witness about any matters on which his instructions differ from the evidence in chief, and about any parts of his case with which the witness can reasonably be expected to deal. Although facts about which the witness has not given evidence in chief are excluded from this rule, the court may draw an adverse inference from failure to cross-examine about a relevant matter with which the witness could have dealt.

It is regarded as unfair to a witness to deny him the opportunity to answer challenges to his evidence, where an advocate intends to invite the court to disbelieve or disregard the evidence of the witness. Accordingly, it is the duty of a cross-examiner to 'put his case' to the witness, or in other words, to question the witness directly on the points on which his evidence diverges from the cross-examiner's instructions. This means that you must fairly put the substance of your case, not that you must harp on every tiny detail. As an advocate, you are trusted to distinguish the essential from the inconsequential. Moreover, it is quite proper to forbear from putting to an exactly corroborative witness everything which you have put to one witness already. It is a safe and good practice to tell the court that, in order to save time and to avoid repetition, you are exercising this discretion.

All advocates are human, and from time to time, you will forget to put something which should be put. When this happens, ask the court to have the witness recalled, if necessary, at the first possible opportunity. Although this can cause delay and inconvenience, it is better than omitting an important aspect of your case. Recall of a witness is within the court's discretion, and although the court may express some disapproval, it will realise that occasional inadvertence is a fact of life. Unless you habitually omit matters and exude a general air of incompetence, you are unlikely to be refused.

Because cross-examination is designed to probe the accuracy of evidence in chief, and to expose dishonest or unreliable evidence, leading questions are always permitted, although many advocates refrain from using them in the interests of cultivating a restrained and moderate style.

The rules of evidence apply to cross-examination, as they do to examination-in-chief, and accordingly questions which invite irrelevant or inadmissible answers may not be asked: *R v Thomson* [11]. However, it is important to take account of a crucial distinction. Although inadmissible evidence may not be elicited in cross-examination, the cross-examiner may freely introduce issues which were not raised, and which perhaps could not have been raised in chief. If such issues are raised, evidence which is relevant to them may become admissible in re-examination, even though it could not have been admitted in chief. Thus, if a witness is asked for the first time in cross-examination about a conversation he had with a third party, the conversation becomes admissible, and the re-examiner may elicit the whole conversation, even though only part of it was introduced in cross-examination. This is a trap into which inexperienced cross-examiners often fall. The conversation may have been wholly inadmissible in chief, but admissible in cross-examination as affecting the credit of the witness. The effect is to allow a full-scale re-examination. A skilled cross-examiner will always consider whether he is letting in evidence on which his opponent may capitalise in re-examination.

Cross-examination on memory-refreshing documents   The above rule is well illustrated by looking at what happens when a cross-examiner cross-examines on a document which a witness has used to refresh his memory while giving evidence. Clearly, such a document is inadmissible as evidence during examination-in-chief, since it is a self-serving document. We have already used the police officer's notebook as a typical example, and it will be convenient to continue to do so, though we have noted that it is in no way distinct from any other contemporaneous document used by any other witness.

The cross-examiner is entitled to inspect in court any memory-refreshing document, but is not obliged to introduce it into evidence. He may forbear from cross-examining on the notebook at all, or cross-examine only on those parts of the notebook used by the officer to refresh his memory, and in neither case does the notebook become evidence. However, once the cross-examiner strays into an area of the notebook to which the officer has not referred to refresh his memory, quite different principles apply. The cross-examination has ceased to be concerned with the memory-refreshing document, and has become concerned with a new documentary item which has not so far formed part of the case. It is just as though the cross-examiner had introduced a document from his own custody and cross-examined the witness about it. The document must go into evidence and be put before the court as a document produced for the purpose of cross-examination, and of course the court may examine the entire document.

For this reason, if there is nothing suspicious or inconsistent on the face of the notebook, the best course is to hand it back to the witness and ask no questions about it. If you do see something which prompts cross-examination, bear the above rule in mind. Ask yourself whether you can exploit any inconsistency without cross-examining on those parts of the notebook to which the officer has not referred. If you cannot avoid this, consider whether the evidential points to be scored by demonstrating the inconsistency are strong enough to justify allowing both the consistent and inconsistent parts of the whole document to go before the bench in evidence. There may be cases in which you are prepared to take this undoubted risk. If the discrepancy between the officer's evidence and the contents of the notebook is substantial and damaging, you may not care that the remainder of the note, which is consistent with his evidence, also goes before the bench. But in the case of an inconsequential or minor discrepancy, you would probably not want to take the risk of having a largely consistent note go before the bench, to provide a permanent record of the officer's evidence.

If the notebook is admitted in evidence as a result of cross-examination, by inadvertence or design, you should still not lose sight of the fact that you are dealing with a memory-refreshing document, and not with a document whose contents have evidential value. At common law, and therefore in criminal cases in the magistrates' court, where a memory-refreshing document is admitted in evidence, it is evidence affecting only the credit of the witness, and is not evidence of the facts contained in the document. In other words, the contents have no evidential value to prove the facts which they record. In *R* v *Virgo* [12], the conviction was quashed where the trial judge directed the jury that the diary of a prosecution witness, which the witness had used to refresh his memory, might be regarded as evidence of the truth of facts contained in the diary. Although the diary had rightly been admitted in evidence, because it had been cross-examined upon extensively, the jury were not entitled to substitute the diary for the evidence of the witness. The diary was evidence affecting only the consistency, and therefore the credit of the witness. In civil cases, s. 3(2) of the Civil Evidence Act 1968 makes a memory-refreshing document evidence of the truth of facts stated in it, as well as evidence of consistency, but its weight on the former issue is generally not great, unless the document is clearly reliable when judged in the light of the circumstances in which it was made, and when compared to the oral evidence of the witness at trial.

Cross-examination concerning credit   The credit, or credibility, of a witness is a factor in the determination by the court of the weight which should be given to his evidence, and will depend on the view which the court takes of his knowledge of the facts, his impartiality, his truthfulness, his respect for his oath or affirmation and his general demeanour. The cross-examiner is entitled to test and to challenge each of these qualities, and is therefore not confined to the facts of the case. The cross-examiner may equally attack the witness in terms of his character, bias or unreliability. The only exception to this is in the case of the defendant in a criminal case, who, as discussed in Chapter 5, is (within certain limits) protected against cross-examination about his previous convictions and bad character by s. 1 of the Criminal Evidence Act 1898.

Even when unrestrained by the rules protecting defendants, it is a good rule of advocacy to refrain from making attacks on the character of witnesses when it can be avoided. In a criminal case, there are specific reasons for this, related to loss of the shield, although cross-examination which exposes the serious bad character of a witness does undoubtedly affect the credit of that witness adversely, and is an accepted, if somewhat over-used weapon. In a civil case, it is almost always a mistake, because a county court judge seeking to decide a case on the balance of probabilities will prefer to avoid viewing character in terms of black and white, and will prefer to find that a witness is mistaken rather than dishonest. A brash attack on the witness will usually forfeit the sympathy of the court. This is especially true where the damage to the witness's credit could equally well have been done by means of demonstrating his unreliability or partiality.

In a criminal case, the court may, as a matter of discretion, restrain and disallow excessive cross-examination concerning credit: *R v Sweet-Escott* [13]. The judge in a civil case probably has the same power, but is more likely to let you carry on and let your forfeiture of his sympathy count against you.

Previous inconsistent statements   A most effective way of attacking the credit of any witness is the use of previous inconsistent statements made by the witness. The use of previous inconsistent statements against one's own hostile witnesses, as permitted by s. 3 of the

Criminal Procedure Act 1865, has been examined in this chapter under the heading 'Unfavourable and hostile witnesses'. Sections 4 and 5 of the same Act make available the same weapon against the other side's witnesses, for which no leave is needed, since one's opponent's witnesses are always deemed to be hostile. These sections, which like s. 3 apply to civil and criminal cases alike, provide as follows:

4. If a witness, upon cross-examination as to a former statement made by him relative to the subject-matter of the indictment or proceeding, and inconsistent with his present testimony, does not distinctly admit that he has made such statement, proof may be given that he did in fact make it; but before such proof can be given the circumstances of the supposed statement, sufficient to designate the particular occasion, must be mentioned to the witness, and he must be asked whether or not he has made such statement.

5. A witness may be cross-examined as to previous statements made by him in writing, or reduced into writing, relative to the subject-matter of the indictment or proceeding, without such writing being shown to him; but if it is intended to contradict such witness by the writing, his attention must, before such contradictory proof can be given, be called to those parts of the writing which are to be used for the purpose of so contradicting him: Provided always that it shall be competent for the judge, at any time during the trial, to require the production of the writing for his inspection, and he may thereupon make such use of it for the purposes of the trial as he may think fit.

Because of the express reference in s. 5 to written statements, s. 4 is generally assumed to refer primarily to previous verbal statements. It is important to follow the procedure laid down by the section. It is necessary to bring to the witness's attention the specific circumstances of the alleged statement, and give him an opportunity to admit or deny making it. If the witness admits to having made the statement, you can than ask why the statement is different from his present evidence. If he denies making the statement, you may prove that the statement was, in fact, made and you can deal with the inconsistency during your closing speech.

Section 5 also calls for more than one step. The first step is to cross-examine the witness without showing him his previous written statement. A frequent error of inexperienced cross-examiners is to rush in and thrust the statement at the witness without preliminaries. You can and should reserve that step until you have obtained an answer to the question whether he made a statement on that occasion or not. Only if you go on to contradict the witness, that is to say, to suggest that his previous statement is true in contradistinction to his evidence at trial, are you obliged to show the witness the statement.

This requires an exercise of judgment on whether you want to go that far, since the court will then see the statement also. Before beginning your cross-examination, you should decide whether you are going to ask the witness to admit that the contents of the previous statement are true, or whether you are content to submit to the court that the witness appears incapable of giving a consistent account of the facts. Always bear in mind that the re-examiner may introduce the whole of the statement for the purpose of re-establishing the credit of the witness, even if you have made use only of part. Make sure that the inconsistency is substantial enough to justify the risk that an otherwise consistent document may be placed before the court. You must, of course, have the written statement available in court for the use of the court, if required.

Despite the reference in s. 5 to the judge making 'such use of [the statement] for the purposes of the trial as he may think fit', the rule at common law for statements adduced under s. 4 or s. 5 is that such statements are evidence affecting only the credit of the witness, and are not evidence of the truth of the facts stated in them. This rule applies to criminal cases in the magistrates' court. In civil cases, s. 3(1)(a) of the Civil Evidence Act 1968 allows such a statement to be used for either purpose, but in keeping with our observations on other analogous situations, it should be noted that the weight of the statement as evidence of the truth of the facts stated in it will not necessarily be very great.

Re-examination and evidence in rebuttal

There are really only two rules of evidence pertaining to re-examination. The first is that leading questions are not permitted. This is for much the same reason as in examination-in-chief, that an advocate should not put words into the mouth of his own witness. The second is that re-examination must be confined to matters raised during cross-examination. This rule is designed to prevent the proliferation and repetition of issues. The art of re-examination, however, as opposed to the rules which govern it, calls for great skill and is much neglected. If you have studied the preceding section dealing with cross-examination, you will probably have begun to appreciate that, when the other side have taken full advantage of the weapons of cross-examination against your witnesses, a certain amount of repair work is necessary. Re-examination is basically a remedial process, but it can also be employed to good effect to emphasise some positive aspect of the witness's evidence, which perhaps was not previously apparent.

This means exploiting every opportunity to put into evidence documents or conversations which were raised for the first time in cross-examination, and knowing when evidence which was inadmissible in chief has become admissible in re-examination. It also requires the advocate to evaluate the damage done to a witness in cross-examination, for example by an attack on character, and to know how to rehabilitate the witness by exploring the facts of previous convictions, or by eliciting mitigating circumstances. If some inconsistency has been exposed by use of a previous inconsistent statement, or some passage in a memory-refreshing document, there is no need to give up altogether. Very often there is some explanation which removes the sting from the cross-examination, and renders innocuous an apparently damaging circumstance. It is your duty as an advocate to monitor the cross-examination of your witnesses with a view to finding such avenues of re-examination. During cross-examination, you should be thinking constantly: 'that sounds bad, but it is not quite like that; why, and what questions can I ask to make the court understand why?'

Evidence in rebuttal is evidence which tends to contradict some evidence called for the other side, but which was not presented during the case of the party calling the evidence. It is a general rule that every party must present all the evidence on which it intends to rely before closing its case. Mere inadvertence does not permit a party to reopen its case once it has been closed, because the other side are entitled to base their conduct of the case on the way in which yours has been presented. This suggests, rightly, that you should draw the attention of the court to any inadvertent omission of relevant evidence at the earliest possible opportunity.

However, the court will allow evidence in rebuttal where any party is taken by surprise by some development during the trial, which necessitates the calling of evidence that could not have been foreseen as necessary at the outset of that party's case. In older cases, such as *R v Frost* [14], it was said that such evidence in rebuttal could be given only if 'any matter arises *ex improviso* which no human ingenuity could foresee'. More modern authority has defined the test as one of reasonable foreseeability, and it seems that evidence may now be introduced to rebut any matter which has genuinely taken a party by surprise. In civil cases, this may often be gauged by what is reasonably to be anticipated on the pleadings, whereas in criminal cases, the question is more one of the court's duty to ensure a fair trial by preventing one side or the other from profiting unfairly by the element of surprise. Leave to call evidence in rebuttal is always required, and will not be granted unless appropriate circumstances can be demonstrated. In *R v Day* [15], a conviction was quashed where the prosecution were permitted to call a handwriting expert, not only after the close of their own case but after the defendant had given evidence, and where it should have been obvious from the outset that such evidence might well be required.

Evidence in rebuttal does not, however, always fall into the category of evidence which might have been introduced during a party's own case. It is sometimes required to rebut answers given during cross-examination, and may have been inadmissible during the cross-examiner's own case. The rule in such cases is that evidence in rebuttal may be called, except in relation to 'collateral issues'. In relation to collateral issues the cross-examiner must accept the answers of the witness as final, not of course in the sense that he cannot challenge them in cross-examination, but in the sense that he cannot introduce evidence in rebuttal to contradict the witness. The rule exists for the purpose of limiting the proliferation of secondary issues which often arise during cross-examination. A collateral issue is one which is not of direct relevance to the outcome of the case, and which, accordingly, could not have been the subject of admissible evidence during the case of the cross-examiner. In *R v Burke* [16], an Irish witness, giving evidence through an interpreter, asserted that he was unable to speak English. He denied in cross-examination that he had spoken English to two persons while in court. This was held to be a collateral issue, and the cross-examiner was not permitted to call evidence in rebuttal to prove that the witness had spoken English. However, the position would have been different if the witness's command of the English language had been directly relevant to some issue in the case, for example, his authorship of a material document or of an alleged confession.

To this so-called rule of finality on collateral issues, there are four exceptions, which should always be borne in mind. These are as follows:

(a) By s. 6 of the Criminal Procedure Act 1865, if a witness denies having been convicted of a criminal offence, or refuses to answer a question on that subject, the conviction may be proved in rebuttal.

(b) Any fact tending to prove bias or partiality on the part of a witness may be proved if denied in cross-examination. Bias or partiality requires a suggestion not just that the witness's evidence is challenged, but that there are specific facts which indicate that the witness is prepared to give evidence untruthfully or unfairly. This may arise from the relationship of the witness to one party or another (for example a mistress: *Thomas* v *David* [17]) or from malice or bribery. But there must be some positive fact; a mere allegation that the witness's evidence is inaccurate, or even untruthful, will not suffice. There must be some positive disposition to favour one side as against the other.

(c) A witness may be called in rebuttal to show that, in the opinion of the witness, a witness called on the other side should not be believed because of his reputation for being unworthy of belief: *R* v *Richardson; R* v *Longman* [18]. Such evidence is rarely used, and probably rarely available, but there is no objection to it. Indeed, the rebutting witness may even state his opinion of the credibility of the opposing witness, provided that the opinion is based on facts within his personal knowledge.

(d) Where evidence is available that, for medical reasons, the reliability of a witness is open to doubt, such medical evidence may be given in rebuttal of the witness's evidence. In *Toohey* v *Commissioner of Police of the Metropolis* [19], the House of Lords held that it was permissible to ask questions of a doctor tending to show that the victim of an alleged offence was abnormally prone to hysteria, and that such hysteria might have been induced by alcohol.

Presentation of documentary and real evidence

Many advocates assume that the presentation of documentary and real evidence involves no more than remembering to bring it to court, together with sufficient copies for the court and other parties. While this is certainly an important consideration, there are less mundane things to think about.

In the case of an evidential document, you must prove, unless admitted, both the contents and, where required, the due execution of the document. Such proof is important in civil cases more often than in criminal, but the rules are the same in either case. Very often, the required proof can be dispensed with by agreement, and you should always invite all other parties to enter into such an agreement in good time before trial.

It is a fundamental and too-often overlooked rule of English law that, in order to prove the contents of an evidential document, primary evidence of those contents must be adduced. In almost all cases, this means producing the original document. An admission by all other parties of the contents of a document is also regarded as primary evidence. In the county court, notice to admit in respect of all evidential documents on which you propose to rely at trial should be served, as provided for by CCR Ord. 20, r. 3(1). Failure of another party to respond with a notice of non-admission will result in such party being deemed to have admitted the authenticity of the documents set forth in your notice. Also regarded as primary evidence is the official copy of a document, the original of which is required by law to be enrolled in a court or other public office. On the other hand, a copy, however produced, and oral evidence about the contents of a document are secondary evidence.

Secondary evidence is admissible to prove the contents of an evidential document only in the following exceptional cases:

(a)   If your opponent fails, after notice to produce, given pursuant to CCR Ord. 20, r. 3(4), to produce at trial the original documents called for, you may prove the contents of such documents by any secondary evidence.

(b)   Secondary evidence may be used to prove the contents of a document where the original is in the lawful possession of a stranger to the proceedings, who refuses and cannot be compelled to produce it. However, if the stranger's possession or refusal to produce is unlawful, the procedure is to compel production of the original, and secondary evidence will not be admissible. For similar reasons, secondary evidence may be admitted where production of the original is physically impossible (for example, where it is a tombstone) or legally impossible (for example where the original is required by law to be kept in or affixed to some public place).

(c)   Where the original has been lost, and cannot be found after all reasonable steps have been taken to search for it (the proof of which lies upon the party asserting the fact) secondary evidence will be admitted.

(d)   The Bankers' Books Evidence Act 1879 provides that a copy of an entry in a banker's book may be admitted as evidence of the contents without production of the original, on certain conditions set forth in the Act designed to ensure the authenticity of the contents and the copy.

Where due execution of a document must be proved, this may be done by direct or percipient evidence of the execution, by the evidence of attesting witnesses, by scientific comparison of the document with a known sample of the handwriting of the purported executer or even by the opinion evidence of a witness familiar with the handwriting of the executer. A document which is, or purports to be more than 20 years old and comes from proper custody, is presumed to have been duly executed. Any document is presumed to have been executed on the date it bears, and except in the case of a will (when the reverse is presumed) it is presumed that any alteration was made before execution.

Where real evidence, such as photographs, tapes and the like, is produced, the party producing it must show a prima facie case that the proposed exhibit is original and authentic. This is a rule of some importance in criminal cases, since the prosecution are often unable, if pressed, to demonstrate a continuous chain of possession of an exhibit such as a tape recording. Since the prosecution must show a prima facie case that the exhibit is the original and has not been tampered with, the court should exclude it if a proper chain of custody cannot be shown and if there is any real possibility of tampering having occurred [20]. This opens up excellent fields of cross-examination, which often reduce the weight of an exhibit, even if the court decides to admit it.

Notes

1.   *Moore v Registrar of Lambeth County Court* [1969] 1 WLR 141; *Tomlinson v Tomlinson* [1980] 1 WLR 323.

2. *Moor* v *Moor* [1954] 1 WLR 927.

3. *R* v *Richardson* [1971] 2 QB 484.

4. (1976) 63 Cr App R 20.

5. (1979) 69 Cr App R 411.

6. [1942] 1 All ER 187.

7. (1971) 56 Cr App R 240.

8. *R* v *Fraser; R* v *Warren* (1956) 40 Cr App R 160.

9. (1976) 64 Cr App R 96.

10. [1972] Crim LR 430.

11. [1912] 3 KB 19.

12. (1978) 67 Cr App R 323.

13. (1971) 55 Cr App R 316.

14. (1840) 9 C & P 129 as reported in 4 St Tr NS 85, 386.

15. [1940] 1 All ER 402.

16. (1858) 8 Cox CC 44.

17. (1836) 7 C & P 350.

18. [1969] 1 QB 299.

19. [1965] AC 595.

20. *R* v *Maqsud Ali* [1966] 1 QB 688; *R* v *Stevenson* [1971] 1 WLR 1.

Nine

Preparing and Presenting a Civil Case

Introduction

The task of the advocate is to persuade and this task calls for a high degree of sensitivity: unfortunately the greater the degree of sensitivity the advocate possesses, the greater is the likelihood of his being nervous at the prospect of advancing his case in court. It is a commonplace at the Bar that many excellent advocates suffer from a high degree of nervousness before going into court. Now a certain degree of nervousness on the part of the advocate is a good thing — in the same way that the good actor will experience such a feeling before going out on to the stage. But every advocate has experienced on some occasion a very different form of nervousness — the panic which destroys what should be a confident performance. In this chapter we intend to suggest how such a failure of confidence can best be avoided; our theme is that even apparently simple litigation merits a great deal of preparation, and that the key to successful advocacy lies not in acquiring some hidden key to eloquence, but in preparing one's case so thoroughly that by the time one arrives at court, a confidence in one's own ability to put over the case will have developed.

The day before the hearing

We start with the preparation the advocate should be making the day or evening before presenting a client's claim in a disputed and somewhat involved case. A good starting-point is to write out a chronology of the relevant events; in a contract case, for example, the negotiations leading up to the agreement, the relevant letters passing between the parties and the meetings when it was appreciated that something was going wrong should all be set out in a logical order of events.

Once the chronology has been prepared the next step is to tie it up with the relevant documents. So, perhaps in a different colour ink, go back over the chronology inserting into it references to the relevant documents. It is worth remembering that many civil cases are won on documents: a judge faced with a conflict of testimony may well decide the case in favour of the party whose account most closely fits in with what is set out in the documents. Therefore at this stage in the preparation of a case, the advocate should be checking that the documentary evidence has been properly prepared. Are the original documents available? If not, have copies been agreed or can it be proved that the original has been destroyed or is missing and reasonable steps have been taken to trace it? There should, of course, have been prepared a bundle of original documents for the use of the witnesses and bundles of paginated copies for the judge and the advocates. It is the responsibility of the plaintiff's solicitor to prepare the bundle for the use of the court; but if you are acting for the defendant and no bundle has been supplied, it may be worth preparing your own; otherwise the plaintiff may profit by the confusion he has created by not putting in a bundle of relevant documentation.

The next step is to read again the proofs of evidence you have taken. Tie up the proofs to the documents. In particular, see whether there is any point at which the evidence of the witness does not appear to tally with the documents; if you find such a point you must take instructions on it. Consider also what passages seem unclear in the proofs — often it is the matter set out in these passages which will be the turning-point of the case, and in these parts of the proofs, the witnesses may seem vague because they have not been totally frank when the proofs were taken.

You will, of course, already have checked that all the relevant witnesses are willing to attend court; if there is any doubt about the matter, you should have issued a witness summons. It is sometimes said that a reluctant witness is not worth calling but we think this is an exaggeration: in truth, there are often many reasons why witnesses who can support your case may be unwilling to attend court and yet, if they do attend, they may give evidence which materially helps you to establish your case. Where, therefore, a witness whose testimony is important is reluctant to attend, often the best course is to issue a witness summons and then check his evidence with him when he arrives at the court. If it is clear at that stage that he is going to be adverse to you, then you can decide not to call him; but if you have not taken this step you may have done your client a great disservice because it may be that if the witness had been prevailed upon to attend he could have won you the case.

We have already discussed the problems peculiar to expert witnesses. By now you must be sure you have understood the evidence your expert will be giving. In particular, you must understand why he says the other side's expert is wrong. Check in this final preparation of the case that your expert has provided you with the necessary outlines for a cross-examination. You will already have seen that a copy of his report, together with the relevant plans and diagrams, is available for the judge. It sometimes happens that in this stage of final preparation of a case your attention is drawn to points in the expert testimony which you have not clarified. Make a written note of these points so that you will be able to check them quickly with your expert before going into court. It is always worth attending court well in advance of the time of the hearing; one reason is that this provides you with a chance of going over these points of evidence, which on a careful final consideration of the case, have suddenly assumed a greater significance than they did earlier on.

The next stage in preparing your note is to consider very carefully what orders you are asking the judge to make. If your case is a claim for damages, are you in a position to prove your loss? It sometimes happens that an advocate will prepare a case perfectly so far as liability is concerned yet fail, or fail to do the best for the client, through not taking sufficient trouble in proving the full extent of the client's loss. The law on damages is complex; you should check, particularly in a contract case, that you understand the measure of damages which is appropriate to the particular claim you are bringing. Never forget the necessity of proving the items of special damage; usually it will be possible to agree these in advance, but where there is no agreement then you should prepare a schedule showing how the relevant sums are calculated. In preparing that schedule, check how you intend to prove each and every item.

If your claim is for damages for personal injuries then go to court with the relevant quantum flagged in Kemp and Kemp on *The Quantum of Damages* and in *Current Law*. Most judges nowadays are prepared to hear an advocate refer to similar cases in order to give the court guidance on the amount to award; there is still, however, a convention that you do not yourself state the sum which you wish the judge to award.

Where you are claiming an order from the court, for example, for an injunction, it is essential that you draft the precise terms of the order so that you can place your draft before the judge.

It is only at this final stage in preparing your note that we recommend you turn to the law. It should have become clear to you what are the points upon which a legal question might arise. Set out in your note references to the appropriate textbooks and statutes and have those books or copies available at court. If it will be necessary for you to refer the judge to a law report or a textbook, make sure that you have a copy available for the judge to read; do not assume that the court will have copies of anything other than the standard official law reports. Nothing is more senseless than reading a report to a judge who has not got a copy and so is not able to follow word by word what you are saying.

At the hearing

It is always a good rule to arrive very early at court — at least three-quarters of an hour before the case is due to be heard. This gives you time for a last conference with your client. It is remarkable how much new material is likely to emerge at this stage — actually arriving at the court door concentrates the client's mind wonderfully. There is another reason why you should arrive early: you must anticipate that at the court door there will be proposals for settlement emanating from the other side; or you yourself may wish at this stage to make proposals to the other side. You must leave yourself ample time to discuss such matters both with your opponent and with your client; many judges are prepared to grant a degree of indulgence to advocates who wish the court to adjourn while terms of settlement are discussed. You should never assume, however, that this will happen and that is why it is worth arriving in time to have these matters sorted out as far as possible before the judge actually sits. It is a very good idea to work out before you arrive at court the minimum terms upon which you would be prepared to settle the case; if these terms are likely to be at all complex, then have them drafted out on paper so that you can discuss them with your opponent and with your client.

Dress correctly for court. It is difficult to persuade a judge to concentrate on your advocacy when he is really thinking with irritation that you have not troubled to dress properly for court. For men, proper court dress involves a dark suit with a waistcoat, a stiff wing-collar and starched clean bands. For women, a black dress and again starched bands are *de rigueur*. You may think these conventions are outdated and senseless but you cannot afford to do anything which could in any way deflect the court's attention from your presentation of your case, and therefore you must accept these rules until at least you are of sufficient seniority for the court not to care whether you have developed eccentricities of dress.

If your case is not the first in the list it is often a good idea to go into court and listen to the earlier cases. If you have not appeared before the judge before, this gives you a chance of forming some assessment of his character. But even if you know the judge well, it may be worth sitting in court for some time just to see what mood he is in today. Judges — even the best judges — are human and like all of us vary from day to day in their temperament. One other point to note; if you do go into the courtroom never be tempted to chatter with the other advocates while another case is going on; judges notice what is happening at the Bar and the sight of advocates talking to each other while waiting for their cases to come on is apt to infuriate them.

At last your case is called on; we will assume that you are acting for the plaintiff and therefore you now rise to make your opening. A good opening can set the tone for the whole case; equally a bad opening may destroy the case before it has even really begun. This is where the value of good preparation becomes apparent. If you have made a note of the sort suggested earlier in this chapter you will have constructed a good opening for your case.

You will start by telling the judge what sort of case this is and what you are claiming; for example, you will say: 'May it please your Honour, this is a claim for damages for breach of contract' or 'This is a claim for possession of a dwelling-house on the grounds of forfeiture for non-payment of rent'. Then move into the chronology of the relevant events.

Imagine, for instance, you are appearing in a simple building dispute. The sensible course is to hand the judge at this stage the bundle of agreed documents and then take him through the chronology tying up each relevant date with the document to which it relates. Thus, for example, you will tell him that on such and such a day the defendant delivered an estimate to the plaintiff, and you will ask the judge to look at the estimate. You will then go on to refer to the dates of the letters which you say together constituted the offer and acceptance of that estimate. You will then go on to give the date when building works began, and then you will itemise the 'extras' by referring to the work which was to be done and the dates, and so you will build up for the judge a chronological picture of the events which he is going to consider in the case. Go slowly at this stage because the judge may well wish to take a note of this chronology of events. When you have completed your outline of the facts and your survey of the documents then turn to the pleadings and any schedule of defects. You can preface your remarks by indicating what you say are the basic issues in the case, for example, whether certain extra work is properly chargeable or whether there has been a breach of certain contractual terms relating to the manner in which various items of work should be done, or whatever it may be. Now ask the judge to look at the pleadings which should set out formally what the issues are. Refer the judge also to any orders that have been made on a pre-trial review or at any other stage in the case, and give the judge the date upon which such orders have been complied with.

It may be at this point in time you will want to amend your pleadings. If so, have a draft of the amended pleading ready to put before the court, and you would be wise to flag in the *County Court Practice* the relevant paragraphs relating to the principles upon which the court gives leave to amend pleadings.

One last word about the opening speech; it is a mistake to write out one's opening verbatim but, since many advocates find that the greatest hurdle to get over is the first words which have to be spoken, there is no reason why you should not write out the first few sentences of your opening remarks and then develop the rest of your opening in note form.

Once the opening is concluded it will be for you, if you are acting for the plaintiff, to call your own client and then the witnesses who support your case. There will be a bundle of original documents before your witness: make sure that at the appropriate moment he produces each of the documents which he can speak about. Remember that if the original is missing, a copy can only be produced if the original has been destroyed or lost (and all reasonable enquiries can be shown to have been made to trace it). When the original is held by the other side you must serve notice on your opponent to produce it.

There are two important rules where one is calling one's own client or one's own witnesses; in taking the client or witnesses through the evidence in chief the advocate is not entitled to lead the witness on any contentious matter. This means the advocate must not ask questions of the witness which suggest the answer the advocate wishes to receive. Thus for example, if it is in dispute that a party agreed to a particular term, it would be quite wrong to lead one's client by asking him, 'Did Mr X say to you such and such?' The proper course when one comes to the matters which are in controversy is simply to ask the witness to explain in his own words what happened or what was said.

The other rule in examining your own client or witnesses is that you are not allowed to contradict their testimony by referring them to any earlier statements they may have made. It will sometimes happen that a witness will depart radically in giving evidence from the proof you have in front of you; you are not in these circumstances entitled to put the witness's proof before him and ask him why he is now saying something different, nor are you entitled to cross-examine him in order to get him to change his testimony. Most advocates in these circumstances will try to ask the question again in case the witness has simply misunderstood them, but once the answer has been clearly given then the advocate must accept that answer and move on to some other point.

Brown's rules

There is a great art in producing the evidence upon which you rely, and many writers on advocacy have said that adducing evidence in chief is a more difficult art than cross-examination. Whether or not that is true, it certainly pays to take great care in the way in which your own evidence is put forward. An American advocate called David Paul Brown formulated in the 19th century certain 'golden rules' for taking a witness through his evidence in chief [1]. These rules contain so much good sense that we think it is worth repeating some of them here.

Brown's first rule relates to the witness who is forward or impertinent; this witness can ruin the presentation of one's case. He demeans the dignity of the court and he may annoy and upset the judge. You as the advocate have to control the witness and prevent him from being forward or impertinent. Brown's suggestion is that you should be very serious and very grave with him; after a few moments he will realise that his impertinence is out of place and is certainly unacceptable to you, and in the vast majority of cases this will affect him sufficiently for his testimony to be given properly.

What you must never do is to go along with such a witness and in any way seek to encourage him.

The second rule that Brown formulated related to the witness who was timid or nervous, and this is a much more common type. Lawyers tend to forget how intimidating it is to a lay person to appear as a witness in a court of law, and your task as the advocate is to make sure that any timidity or nervousness on the part of your witness does not prevent him from giving the testimony for which you have called him. Therefore, says Brown, it is worth beginning by asking the witness about familiar matters and lead him only gradually to the questions which are contentious and upon which you expect he will later be cross-examined. So, for example, if in a case involving a factory accident you were calling a particular workman, it would be worth asking him about his job, his duties and about how long he had been employed before one turned to the facts of the accident. Most judges understand why this is done and will not criticise the advocate for attempting shortly to make the witness feel at home.

The third witness identified by Brown was the witness who was unfavourable; by that is meant the witness who says something which strikes against the case you are trying to build up. It is an important rule that one should not at this stage appear to be taken aback. This is particularly true where the tribunal consists of lay persons, for example, an industrial tribunal or magistrates, but it is also true of the judge; all tribunals watch the advocate and all advocates therefore have to develop devices of their own for concealing the fact that a witness's testimony may have come as a very unpleasant shock to them.

The fourth type of witness, says Brown, is the witness who is prejudiced. By this he means the witness who is obviously hostile to your client. Normally in such a case the only advice that can be given is not to call that witness, but sometimes the witness has to be called, and you have no alternative, because he is going to give some item of evidence which is essential so far as your case is concerned. The advice in such a case is to get rid of him from the witness-box as quickly as possible; certainly do not think that you will be able to charm him while he is in the witness-box into helping your case. The only safe course is to ask him shortly the matters upon which he gives vital testimony and then sit down.

Brown's fifth rule relates to the witness whom your adversary must call. You should never call such a witness, the reason being that if you let the other side call him you will be able to cross-examine him, and cross-examination, particularly of a witness who is not hostile to your case, is a far easier method of eliciting the evidence that you want to present before the court than examination-in-chief.

Brown's sixth rule is never to ask a witness a question without some object. We would also suggest that you should consciously try not to ask questions which can be objected to. Of course this is a counsel of perfection because every advocate from time to time will make a mistake, but one should think about the admissibility of the evidence that one proposes to adduce, and although a court will forgive one or perhaps two mistakes, the advocate who is constantly asking improper questions will forfeit the confidence of the court.

We would add to Brown's rule the suggestion that you should not object to your opponent's questions unless the matters involved are crucial to the case. There is nothing which irritates the tribunal more than the advocate who keeps on taking points of evidence where the matters in question are not of any great significance. Therefore confine your objections to the occasions when the other side have asked the witness to give inadmissible evidence about matters which are really crucial to the case. When such a matter does arise and you have made your objection, you must then be prepared to argue distinctly and without hesitation why the evidence is not admissible. This is why a thorough and readily accessible knowledge of the basic rules of evidence is of such great assistance to the advocate. Questions of the admissibility of evidence arise suddenly during the course of a case and cannot always be anticipated. The good advocate knows this and is able to explain clearly and distinctly why it is that he objects to any matter of evidence.

The last of Brown's rules seems almost self-evident, and yet it is often seen to be broken in practice. Brown says that the advocate must speak clearly and distinctly as if he is awake and engaged in a matter of interest. There is nothing more unattractive than the advocate who appears to be bored with the case upon which he is engaged, and yet many advocates affect such a lack of interest. This is an unattractive approach to advocacy and we would suggest that the good advocate is the advocate who is seen to be clearly concerned and interested in the case which he is advancing.

We would add to Brown's rules one overriding principle, and that is that the advocate should be polite. It sometimes seems to a lay person that lawyers are unduly obsequious in court. In truth, they are taking part in a highly organised ritual, where the use of language is important, and where deference to the tribunal expressed in the language used actually assists in making the process work. It may be very difficult to restrain one's temper in the face of a witness who is being hostile or rude, and indeed every advocate has come across the occasion when judges have been less than courteous to him; nonetheless we believe that it is of paramount importance that the advocate should always be seen to be courteous and polite both to the witnesses and to the tribunal.

During your opponent's cross-examination

When the examination-in-chief is concluded you sit down and your opponent begins to cross-examine your witness. You must take a very full and careful note of the cross-examination. Take down as much as you possibly can because it is often not apparent at any given moment whether or not the particular passage of evidence will subsequently appear to be important. The judge will himself take a note of both the evidence in chief and cross-examination, and most judges like the advocates to refer to the evidence by referring to a note; one only has to sit in a county court for a day to see the number of occasions in a contested trial in which the judge will refer back to the notes he has taken, and ask the advocates to refer to the notes they have of the relevant passages. Quite apart from this it must be remembered that many cases in the county courts are adjourned either for further evidence or for argument, and it is of great help to the advocate to have a full note of evidence when days or weeks later he comes to prepare the case again for the next stage of the hearing.

Your own cross-examination

The rules of evidence so far as cross-examination are concerned are straightforward; the advocate is entitled to ask as many leading questions as he wishes in cross-examination and he is entitled to put to the witness any letter or note or other document in which the witness has earlier said something different from the testimony he has given in the witness-box. Although the rules of evidence are straightforward, the actual technique of cross-examination is difficult and sometimes, to the beginner, extremely difficult. We offer some suggestions. The first thing to do is to determine whether the witness who has given evidence which is adverse to your client is merely mistaken or is deliberately fabricating the evidence. In 90 per cent or more of all cases (particularly in civil courts) witnesses are in fact mistaken and not lying when they give evidence which is subsequently rejected by the court. It is much easier to persuade a judge that a witness is mistaken than that he is lying. Now if you come to the conclusion that the witness who has said something adverse to your client has made a genuine mistake, the right course in cross-examining him is to indicate to him at the very beginning of your questioning that you are not suggesting that he is lying; this often comes as a great relief to the witness who, on the basis of television dramas and novels, will have an exaggerated idea of what is likely to happen to him in the witness-box. Once you have made it clear to the witness that it is not part of your case that he is in any way dishonest, he will automatically be relieved and more amenable to the suggestions that you put to him.

There is not much point in this stage in putting it squarely to the witness that he is wrong, because all of us have a natural pride in our memory and in our ability to comprehend what has been going on and would resent such a frontal attack. The best technique with such a witness is to explore with him in more detail the surrounding circumstances of the disputed matter upon which he has given evidence, and in exploring those circumstances see if in his account of the detail of the events in question he is putting forward a version of events which contains inconsistencies, or which is simply on a balance of probability unlikely to be true. Often it will be very relevant to see if his detailed account under cross-examination ties up with what has been recorded at the time in relevant documents.

When, as will be rare in a civil case, you come to the conclusion that the witness is lying, then the technique of cross-examination will be rather different. You should out of fairness make it clear to the witness that you do not accept his testimony is truthful. That does not, however, mean that you should cross-examine crossly or in an impolite manner. The method of cross-examination is to keep testing his story by making him repeat the evidence that he has given in the witness-box and asking for details. Many a man can invent a simple story but few have the imagination to be able to colour it with detail, and one of the techniques of cross-examining a lying witness is to demonstrate, by pressing him for the detail of his story, that his evidence cannot be true. Expect in such a case the witness to become evasive. If he does so, you must not allow him to avoid answering the question. One characteristic of untruthful witnesses is that when they see a question which they think might expose their dishonesty they will answer some other question, or embark upon a long involved story which detracts from the question that has been put to them. Be careful to watch out for such behaviour.

Final speech

At the end of the evidence you will be called upon to make your final speech. Now in a civil action this is more difficult to prepare than in a criminal case; you will be addressing a professional lawyer who will not be at all interested in any sort of flight of rhetoric; he will also expect something more than a prepared statement of your case. In the final speech you have to be flexible and you have to look back at the evidence that has been given. Remember of course that in a civil case the party wins whose version of events is more likely to be correct than his opponent's — i.e., he succeeds on a 'balance of probabilities'. You are arguing therefore that your account is more likely to be true than the other side's. The speech will therefore be very different from that of a criminal advocate seeking to show there is a reasonable doubt about the matter.

It is often a sensible starting-point to ask the judge to look at the facts which are not in dispute and to show that those agreed facts are more consistent with your client's explanation of the matters than the explanation put forward by the other side. Another valid method of argument at this stage is to ask the judge to prefer the oral evidence which has been supported by the documents rather than the evidence which is either unsupported or indeed contradicted by what has been contained in the documentation.

The advocate should tell the judge what facts he asks him to find. It is important at this stage to use to the judge the correct language of advocacy; the advocate will 'submit' to the judge. It is unprofessional to tell the judge what you 'think' or what you 'believe'.

Above all, it is important both in your final speech and throughout the conduct of the case to be yourself; inexperienced advocates sometimes imagine that they should put on some completely different personality in order to impress the court; nothing could be more silly. The advocate who is attractive is the advocate who is sincere and unaffected. By sincerity we do not mean that the advocate has to believe what his client has told him; but what he must do is to suspend any disbelief that he has once he has clear instructions about the way a case should proceed, and he must present his client's case in a manner which makes it clear that it is a version of events sincerely put forward to the court.

Finally, at this stage, may we point out that every advocate requires a high degree of courage if he is to succeed. It takes courage to appear at all in a public forum; most tribunals are aware of the difficulties of advocacy, and the typical judge today behaves with courtesy and consideration, particularly to the young advocates who are appearing before him. But every advocate on occasion has the misfortune to come before a judge who, for one reason or another, is bad tempered or is acting in a boorish manner; in these very trying circumstances the good advocate has to keep his end up and must, while remaining courteous to the tribunal, insist on behalf of his client that his case is properly heard. This requires a very high degree of courage and is one of the reasons why advocacy properly commands a high degree of respect from the public.

Note

1. The complete text of David Paul Brown's rules is to be found in Sir Frederic Wrottesley, *The Examination of Witnesses in Court*, 3rd ed. (London, 1961). The book is unfortunately now out of print but copies appear from time to time in bookshops and are well worth purchasing.

Ten

Preparing and Presenting a Criminal Case

Introduction

Even if you never intend to set foot in a civil court, and regard yourself as a confirmed criminal practitioner, we recommend that if you have not already done so, you read Chapter 9 of this book before proceeding further with this chapter. While there are certainly important differences of approach to advocacy as between civil and criminal cases, there is also a sense in which advocacy is a single art, and much that was said in Chapter 9 concerning general principles of good advocacy in civil cases is applicable equally to criminal cases in the magistrates' court. Good advocacy always takes account of the nature of the tribunal before which it is conducted, and you will naturally adapt any principle of advocacy to the extent necessary to conform to the requirements of the court in which you are appearing. However, it is surprising how much the successful advocate relies upon well-tried techniques, whatever the tribunal.

It is important in criminal cases no less than in civil cases to prepare well in advance of trial, and to prepare as thoroughly as you possibly can by arranging your papers, documents and exhibits in a logical sequence and by achieving a mastery of the facts and chronology of the case. It is also just as important to arrive at court in ample time, to spend time in court before your case is called on, so as to allow yourself time to assess the bench or the mood of the bench, and to conduct yourself in court in a professional and becoming manner. These are fundamental principles of good advocacy applicable to any case, and need not be repeated here.

A word must be said about two subjects — manner of dress and manner of addressing the court — on which, although the principles good advocacy are the same, the detail must vary as between the county court and the magistrates' court.

Despite the apparently wide divergence of dress seen in magistrates' courts up and down the country, we recommend a conservative appearance for the advocate. Since robes are not worn in the magistrates' court, the anonymity of the uniform of gown, bands and wing collar (and wig, if applicable) cannot be relied upon to achieve the desired result. Your dress will, therefore, convey far more about you than would a mere disposition towards neatness in terms of a clean gown and starched bands. The safe rule for men is to wear a dark (i.e., black, grey or very dark blue) three-piece suit, in which definition we would include the traditional black jacket and waistcoat with pin-striped trousers. For women, we would recommend a formal suit or dress with high neck and long sleeves, in the same colours. The object, of course, is not to distract the court from your advocacy by offering it any excuse for pre-occupation with your appearance.

In the county court, the judge is addressed as 'your honour'. Would that such simplicity were recognised in the magistrates' court, for it should be. The correct mode of address to a bench of magistrates is not to the bench at all, but to the chairman or chairwoman, who is addressed as 'sir' or 'madam', as the case may be. The remaining magistrates need not be addressed directly, although it is good advocacy to refer to them occasionally as the 'colleagues' of the chairman or chairwoman, to show that you have not forgotten them. The appellation, 'your worships', so beloved of police officers, is inappropriate when used by professional advocates and sometimes irritates benches in London and other cities. It is particularly tactless to use it on a stipendiary magistrate sitting in the singular rather than the plural. One really undesirable appellation is that which describes the magistrates as 'learned'. This is a term of art for referring to members of the Bar or judges, and its abuse is, strangely, often resented by magistrates. It is permissible and courteous, although not strictly necessary, to use the word 'learned' when referring to the clerk. As with dress, the object of using correct forms of address is to avoid distracting the bench from your advocacy by focusing their attention on peripheral matters.

The concept of the ideal closing speech

We recommend an approach to preparing criminal cases which may, at first sight, appear eccentric. It is based on the concept of the ideal closing speech, that is to say the closing speech which you, as an advocate, would ideally like to make, if the evidence given in your case were actually to justify it. The concept can be applied to an opening speech, but is at its clearest when applied to a closing speech. Since the prosecution have no right to a closing speech in the magistrates' court, except for the limited purpose of responding to points of law, we shall, for the purposes of illustration, concentrate on the defence closing speech.

The concept is apparently eccentric because it seems premature to sit down before trial, before any evidence is given, to write a closing speech. This, however, is where the word 'ideal' comes into play. The point is that to compose the strongest possible closing speech, the most persuasive argument to the court that you can imagine on the basis of your client's instructions, serves to focus your mind on the evidence which would be required to put you in a position to make it. This does not mean, of course, that you will be able to obtain the required evidence, or that, even if you can obtain it, it will necessarily underwrite every point you would ideally wish to make. But it does provide you with a useful summary of the direction in which your trial preparation should go — what witnesses must be interviewed, whether character witnesses should be sought, how you will approach the prosecution witnesses and any co-defendants in cross-examination, whether a plan or photographs or other similar visual aids would be useful, and a myriad of other matters. By preparing your ideal closing speech, you have forced yourself to think about what you need in terms of evidence for the effective presentation of your case. You have also, incidentally, created an invaluable note to take to court, which will, when amended to take account of the evidence actually given, provide an excellent framework for the speech you will in fact make.

Gathering the evidence

One thing which should emerge with some clarity from your ideal closing speech is a picture of the witnesses you will need to call at trial. If you are prosecuting, you will have been provided with statements from the available witnesses, and can usually assume that no others are known. As a defender, you have to be more resourceful. At the outset of your involvement with the case, you may know of no witnesses apart from the defendant. Your first task will be to ascertain whether the defendant knows of any witnesses who might help. Having read Chapter 6, you will appreciate that, in addition to any factual witnesses, you should always consider whether expert or character witnesses might be desirable. Make sure that you locate and take a proof of evidence from all likely witnesses in good time. It is a serious error to leave this until the day before trial. For one thing, you do not know whether you may have to issue a witness summons to compel attendance. For another, what they have to tell you may suggest the need for further investigation. You may need to take further instructions from the defendant for use in conjunction with the evidence of the witnesses. Make sure that you have access to any useful documents or exhibits that the witnesses may have. Expert and character witnesses can often be difficult to find, since the quality of both is particularly important, and the need for prompt action is acute in their cases.

There is no property in a witness. In some cases, you will feel that a proposed witness for the prosecution should be interviewed. There is no reason why this should not be done, but there are guidelines. A Law Society ruling requires that you notify the police of your intention, and afford them the opportunity to be present. We also recommend that, whenever possible, you arrange for an independent solicitor to be present.

Gaining access to the prosecution evidence in other respects prior to trial is more problematic. One vexing and continually recurring question is whether you will be given a sight of the prosecution statements before the trial commences. Section 48 of the Criminal Law Act 1977 empowers the Lord Chancellor to make rules to ensure that the defence 'is furnished with, or can obtain, advance information concerning all, or any prescribed class of, the facts and matters of which the prosecutor proposes to adduce evidence', and to require a magistrates' court to adjourn a case pending compliance with such rules, 'unless . . . satisfied that the conduct of the case for the accused will not be substantially prejudiced by non-compliance'. At the time of writing, no rules have been promulgated under this section, and the defence remain at the mercy of prosecutors, whose practice varies widely. There is as yet no right to see the prosecution statements prior to summary trial, and intransigent prosecutors can, and often do, refuse this. There are, nonetheless, methods of persuasion. One is to go armed with the text of s. 48 and appeal to the prosecutor's better nature by inviting him to comply with the expressed intention of the legislature. If this fails, try explaining to the prosecutor that you may have to interrupt the trial at frequent intervals to take instructions if taken by surprise by the evidence. If this fails, do so, and explain apologetically to the bench why it is necessary. Bear in mind that if the offence is one triable either way, you are entitled to see the statements on electing trial on indictment.

There is a general duty on the prosecution to inform the defence of the known previous convictions of a prosecution witness, and it is always proper for a defender to enquire about them before the trial begins. There are further duties on the prosecution to make available as a witness for the defence any person from whom they have taken a statement, and know to be capable of giving material evidence, but do not propose to call as a prosecution witness, and to advise the defence of any material inconsistency between the evidence given by a prosecution witness and a previous statement made by the witness to the prosecution. Neither duty obliges the prosecution actually to supply the defence with a copy of the witness's statement.

You are entitled to see the original of any exhibit which the prosecution intend to produce as evidence at trial, including any statement under caution made by your client. For the reasons discussed in Chapter 4, you should always avail yourself of this opportunity. You are also entitled to see the charge sheet, which surprisingly often proves to be a mine of useful information about times and places, and your client's possessions at the time of his arrest. The police will often, on request, allow you or your expert witness to inspect under supervision such exhibits as photographs, tapes and material objects. One object of this, quite apart from affording you and your expert witness access to the exhibits, is to check their originality and authenticity. There should be an unbroken chain of possession of exhibits which ensures that they can be positively identified as being what they purport to be, and that they have not been altered or tampered with. Unless the party producing an exhibit can demonstrate at least a prima facie case that this is so, the court should refuse to admit the exhibit into evidence. This is often of great significance when dealing with tapes, photographs, video-tapes and the like, but is often ignored when cross-examination of the custodians of the evidence would yield promising results. A pre-trial view of the exhibits, with your expert if appropriate, often opens up lines of inquiry.

You should give some thought to preparing exhibits of your own. The use of photographs, plans, models and the like appears, for some reason, to be almost a prosecution prerogative. To ignore the possibilities of such demonstrative evidence is to ignore a potent forensic weapon, since it often conveys relevant facts to a court far more vividly than argument or oral evidence. When confronted with some illustrative device of this kind, the bench feel, understandably, more closely involved with the presentation of the case. They may also feel that a case which has been prepared with such care and forethought must command some credibility. It is surprising how little effort is really involved in the preparation of good photographs and other similar exhibits. As items of real evidence, they are admissible subject only to authentication, that is to say calling evidence from the maker of each exhibit to establish its originality and freedom from tampering and falsification.

Preparation of cross-examination

It is a trite saying, but a true one, that cross-examination is one of the most difficult arts that can confront the advocate in any court. Whole treatises have been written on the supposed techniques of cross-examination. Much of what has been written, while perfectly valid, relates to the colourful and theatrical style of cross-examination which is popularly supposed to be effective in front of a jury. In this day and age, it is doubtful whether such flamboyance of style is effective before any tribunal, and before a county court judge, a stipendiary magistrate or even an experienced lay bench, it may justly be compared to playing the second house at the Barnsley music-hall on a wet Monday evening.

We shall, therefore, confine ourselves to some very simple, but effective rules which govern good cross-examination under any circumstances. These rules will not make you into another Marshall Hall, for it is very difficult to say what makes the difference between a competent technician and a true artist in the field of cross-examination, but they should prevent you from making at any rate the most obvious and dire errors. Our rules are four in number:

(a) Decide what kind of witness you have to cross-examine. Like all advocacy, cross-examination depends first and foremost upon good preparation. This is easier if you have access to the prosecution statements before trial, but in any case a certain degree of preparation is possible on the basis of your instructions. The most fundamental decision you must make, based on your instructions, the statement if you have it, and the demeanour of the witness while giving evidence in chief is whether the witness is (i) dishonest, (ii) unreliable or (iii) mistaken, or whether the witness perhaps falls into some other category of your own invention. The importance of this decision, which must often be made very quickly, cannot be overstated. Firstly, on it depends whether your client may lose his shield because you have, in cross-examination, made an imputation on the character of the witness within the meaning of s. 1(f)(ii) of the Criminal Evidence Act 1898. In many cases you will have no choice. If your instructions are that 15 minutes' worth of alleged verbal admissions were never said at all, it is no good trying to suggest to the officer that he is mistaken about it. The allegation is one of perjury or fabrication of evidence, which is always an imputation on character. But more often, your instructions are consistent with unreliability or mistake, and these can be asserted without loss of the shield. Secondly, your classification of the witness is bound to govern the style of your cross-examination, and you must have clear in your mind, before you begin to cross-examine, what it is you hope to achieve. If the witness can be cross-examined satisfactorily as a category (ii) or category (iii) witness, why risk alienating the bench by setting out to prove that he is a liar falling squarely within category (i)? Benches, quite naturally, much prefer to avoid finding somebody to be a liar if it is possible that he is simply unreliable or mistaken.

(b) Keep aggression to a minimum. This rule follows from the first. Aggression is rarely commendable in a cross-examiner, and even when called for, requires great skill to execute properly. It is unforgivable for an advocate to harass, intimidate or argue with a witness, or to appear to do any of these things. Firmness is acceptable, as is persistence, but these qualities may be demonstrated without aggression. Unless you have committed yourself to a classification of the witness as falling within category (i), a reasonable, enquiring style is invariably more effective, and reduces the risk both of alienating the bench and of accidentally losing your client's shield. You only have to spend a little time watching the best cross-examiners at the Bar to appreciate how much more effective is a quiet, methodical approach than an all-out assault.

(c)   Deal first with non-contentious matters. This rule stems from the fact that cross-examination has two purposes, and not just one. These were described in Chapter 8. Many advocates concentrate on the purpose of challenging the evidence in chief, to the exclusion of the purpose of eliciting facts favourable to the case of the cross-examiner, which have not emerged or which were insufficiently emphasised in chief. If you know that you will have to challenge certain evidence given by the witness, you may wish to divide your cross-examination into two phases. The first phase should be non-contentious. In this phase, you will be gathering facts about which the witness will not object to telling you. Only later will you move into phase two, the challenging phase, at the moment when you feel that the witness has given you all the voluntary assistance he is likely to give you. The consequence of reversing the order of these phases is, of course, that the witness will already feel hostile by the time you tone down your cross-examination to the non-contentious level, and is unlikely to give you much assistance.

(d)   Never ask an unnecessary question. The object of all examination of witnesses is to elicit sufficient evidence to build the foundation of your closing speech. One of the advantages of having prepared your ideal closing speech is that you should know what evidence you need in order to make the desired submissions. When you have gathered this evidence, stop. It is rightly said that one of the most difficult things for an advocate to learn is to shut up and sit down. Certainly, it can be a real exercise in self-discipline when the client is sitting behind you willing you to take the other side's witnesses on, and expecting to get his, or the Legal Aid Fund's money's worth in terms of forensic action. But the lesson is also one of the most important of all to learn, because many are the cases that are ruined by that one question too many. This is particularly critical in cross-examination, when it must be assumed that the witnesses on the other side are hostile. If a witness has not harmed your case, it is best not to cross-examine at all, unless you wish to bring out non-contentious facts. If you have to go further, it is a good working rule to confine cross-examination to the minimum necessary to put your case properly. Avoid the temptation to 'hammer home' some point which the witness may have made which is favourable to you; given a second chance, the witness may withdraw or qualify his answer and take away your advantage. The proper time to hammer a point home is in your closing speech, when the danger from witnesses has passed.

Never ask a witness to probe your client's state of mind; 'You have no reason to believe my client was dishonest, have you?' and the like gives the witness a standing invitation to sink you without trace. It is an unnecessary, and strictly inadmissible question (though your opponent is unlikely to object) since the witness does not know what your client's state of mind was, and his speculation on the subject is unlikely to help you.

Do not ask a witness to explain his reason for doing something, unless it is unavoidable, and it usually is. The classic here is, 'Officer, why were you following my client?' The officer will eventually overcome his professional inhibitions and tell you, and since you asked him, it will sound pretty lame when you object that the answer is inadmissible. In summary, ask yourself constantly: have I now enough to make the points which I want to make in my closing speech, based on this witness's evidence? At the first moment when the answer to that question is in the affirmative, sit down and wait for the opportunity to make those points. Do not try to score additional points off the witness. You are much more likely to lose those you already have.

Preparing the defendant's evidence in chief

Chapter 9 has dealt already with a number of important matters concerning the technique of conducting an examination-in-chief. These are applicable to criminal trials just as much as to civil, and repay constant study and application. They can be applied to the evidence of the defendant and of any other witness, whether factual, expert or character, whom you may determine to call as a result of preparing your ideal closing speech. To that extent, we need not consider the evidence of the defendant as a separate subject. However, the evidence of the defendant sometimes calls for additional exercises in judgment, the theoretical basis for which has already been explored in previous chapters.

The first point on which the advocate's judgment is required derives from the fact that the defendant is not obliged to give evidence in his defence at all. Although competent, the defendant is not a compellable witness. Moreover, because of the burden and standard of proof in criminal cases, the defendant may simply remain silent and say to the prosecution, in effect, 'You have not proved your case; there is nothing for me to answer.' While this is all very well in theory, and sometimes works well in front of a jury, it is rarely a practical proposition in the magistrates' court, where the bench, as a broad matter of common sense, will inevitably find it suspicious if the defendant does not tell them his side of the story from the witness-box. There used to be an alternative, which again was always more effective in front of a jury, of having the defendant make an unsworn statement from the dock, on which he could not be cross-examined. However, this right was abolished by s. 72 of the Criminal Justice Act 1982. The choice now, therefore, is between calling the defendant and not calling him. The choice is that of the defendant, not his advocate, but the defendant will almost always accept his advocate's advice on this matter, and in the magistrates' court, that advice should be to give evidence except in the rarest of cases. Such a case would probably only arise when the bench have agonised over a submission of no case to answer, and clearly regard the prosecution case as extremely weak. In this rare type of case, a decision not to call the defendant sometimes pushes the bench over the edge after your closing speech, and also avoids the possibility that the defendant may supply a case against himself which the prosecution have been unable to supply —a by no means unusual event in criminal trials.

The other major factor in planning the defendant's evidence in chief relates to his previous character. If the defendant is of good character, this fact should be brought out in cross-examination of the officer in charge of the case, by calling the defendant to say so and by calling a reputable and credible character witness, if one is available. As was said in Chapter 5, evidence of good character not only assists the credit of the defendant as a witness, but is actually some evidence tending to show that he is innocent.

Representing a client of previous bad character presents some difficult choices. Naturally, magistrates need little experience to realise the significance of a discreet silence about previous character during a trial. Nonetheless, it is a sound rule which should be followed in almost every case, that the defendant's bad character should be withheld from the bench whenever possible. Magistrates are quite used to suppressing the urge to speculate about the defendant's character, as it is in most cases a very difficult area in which to speculate, and they habitually decide cases without giving the subject a thought.

There are, however, some cases in which the voluntary revelation of the defendant's character may be advantageous, at least when compared to the alternatives. For example, where your client has undoubtedly lost his shield, the prosecutor will not agree to withhold cross-examination about character and you have no real argument for discretion, the best course is probably to introduce your client's character in chief. Unpalatable as this may be, it is generally better than waiting for it to be dragged out in cross-examination. This is designed to, and often does, take the wind out of the prosecutor's sails.

Another example is found in what we shall call in this book — it is not a known technical term — the doctrine of relative good character. The doctrine of relative good character comes into play when the client's previous character, though from a technical standpoint bad, is in some way sympathetic. The former rogue who has gone straight for many years offers one illustration, since his abstention from crime for a substantial time suggests an honest nature. The doctrine trades the defendant's right to withhold his character for the credit gained for frankness with the court. It may be applied where the defendant's bad character is concerned with offences of a radically different nature from that charged. A defendant charged with indecent assault on a child who volunteers his total criminal record consisting of a few convictions for theft may not only be gaining credit for frankness, but also asserting his lack of propensity to commit sexual offences. Sometimes a defendant with a record for similar offences may be well advised to reveal his character, where he has always readily admitted his guilt in the past by a plea of guilty.

The doctrine of relative good character is not an every-day weapon, but is to be used sparingly and with good judgment. There are also two essential steps to take before using it. The first is to check the defendant's record in meticulous detail. Nothing is worse than finding out too late that the defendant's record is far worse, or of a different nature than the defendant told you, and defendants do forget the details from time to time. The second is to explain to the defendant what you propose to do, and obtain his informed consent to the surrender of an important right. A sudden and unexpected allusion to bad character from one's own advocate in court tends to injure the always fragile relationship of trust between advocate and client.

Lastly, always consider the likely effect of the defendant's evidence on any co-defendants. Remember that if the defendant gives evidence against a co-defendant, he loses his shield with even more certainty than he does by making imputations on the character of prosecution witnesses. If the case inevitably involves a 'cut-throat' defence, fate leaves you no real choice but to ask the defendant questions which implicate the co-defendant, and this is quite enough to lose you your shield. But in cases where your defence does not depend upon implicating the co-defendant, make sure that your client does not launch a gratuitous attack on the co-defendant. It is bad enough to lose the shield in a good cause; to lose it unnecessarily is terrible.

All these considerations regarding the defendant's evidence require you to spend time with the defendant before the trial, explaining to him the principles involved and winning his confidence in the decisions you propose to take which will call for his co-operation as a witness. It is by no means a bad thing to give the defendant a 'dry run' through his evidence in chief in your office, before trial. Not only will it boost your client's confidence and hopefully improve his performance in the witness-box, but because of its immediacy, it is also a first-rate was of getting further. instructions and warning yourself about the answers you are likely to receive in court. You would not be the first advocate to scrap and remodel in its entirety a proposed examination-in-chief after conducting a session of this kind.

Preparing and delivering your speech

The ability to make a good speech is the key to persuasion in advocacy. The word advocacy derives from the Latin '*ad vocare*', meaning literally 'to call towards'. Advocacy is, then, the art of winning the listener over to the advocate's cause by persuasive speaking. Although every aspect of the advocate's presence in court, including the presentation of evidence, should be directed to this end, it is generally accepted that the art comes into its own most strongly in the making of a speech to the bench, judge or jury. We shall consider briefly three kinds of speech relevant to criminal trials, namely the opening speech, the submission of no case to answer and the closing speech. But it is appropriate to preface this discussion by one or two observations concerning style.

The best style to adopt in making any speech is your own. While there is nothing wrong with picking up useful techniques and phrases from other experienced advocates, an attempt to imitate the style of another is doomed to failure. The techniques you will learn by experience and by listening to others can be built into your style; no good advocate ever stops learning new techniques of speech or developing new ideas. Because the object is to persuade the court before which you are appearing, you will mould the content of the speech to be as pleasing to the court as possible. Your speech to a stipendiary magistrate should be very different from your speech to a lay bench on the same facts. Your speech to a bench known to you from long association with the court should be different from your speech to an unfamiliar bench on the same facts. In the same way, of course, in your local county court, your speech to Judge A who sits on Mondays should be different from your speech to Judge B who sits on Tuesdays. If, one Monday, Judge A is indisposed and you come before Judge B unexpectedly, you should make some swift revisions to your planned speech.

Of course, a primary reason for our recommendation that you spend time in court before your case is called on, is that it is important to find out as much as you can in that limited time about the bench, its attitudes, forensic taste and even its mood. The opportunity for such observation may be limited, but any information is better than none. The advantage of the local advocate appearing before a familiar local bench is considerable in this respect, and having such an advocate as your opponent in a strange court can put you at a disadvantage which should not be underestimated. In any court, it is a sound rule to be as brief as is consistent with a full presentation of your arguments. Not only does brevity always commend itself to a busy court, but it also reduces the risk that the impact of what you say, your persuasiveness, may be eroded by overstretching the attention span of the tribunal.

The purpose of an opening speech, whether made for the prosecution or, in very rare cases for the defence, is simply to give the court an overview of the evidence which is to follow, together with a short statement of the applicable law. It is almost always a mistake to make an opening speech for the defence. The nature of most defences appears quite clearly from the path taken in cross-examination, and only in a complex case involving a number of witnesses or very difficult evidence should an opening speech be contemplated. In all other cases, a defence opening speech is no more than an unnecessary risk that your right to make a closing speech, your real chance to be persuasive, will be lost. For the prosecution, conversely, the opening speech is the best opportunity to be persuasive. Some prosecutors forbear from making an opening speech in simple cases, but the best course would seem to make a speech of a brevity proportionate to the simplicity of the case. Brevity is always desirable in an opening. Unlike juries, magistrates do not need an exhaustive explanation of all the facts. Try to develop an outline of the salient facts and law, leaving the detail to emerge during the evidence. It gives an impression of disorganisation to seem to be reading the anticipated evidence directly from the statements, particularly if this involves a recitation of lengthy interviews. It is always far better not to read from any statement, and to make a concise summary of the anticipated evidence in your own words. An orderly presentation of the salient points will be clear and persuasive in itself. Omit from an opening speech any evidence which you are told by your opponent is alleged to be inadmissible. The procedure for dealing with this is described in Chapter 1.

A submission of no case to answer is made at the close of the prosecution case, and before any presentation of the defence case. Such a submission must be based either on the fact that there is no evidence to prove an essential element of the offence charged, or on a submission that the prosecution evidence has been so discredited by cross-examination, or is so manifestly unreliable that no reasonable tribunal could safely convict on it. What you say must, therefore, be directed to explaining to the bench why the case falls under one or both of those heads.

It is always a good beginning to remind the bench of the object of your submission, and to emphasise that because of the burden and standard of proof in criminal cases, they not only may, but should dismiss the charge without calling on the defence in a proper case. The great rule about submissions of no case is to make them only in cases where there is a reasonable prospect of success. Remember that if you fail, the case goes on, and you would much prefer not to have to go on with a bench profoundly irritated by having to sit through a hopeless submission. If the case presents a submission which, though not of the strongest, should be made, make it with truly exemplary brevity. A well made submission, based on plausible grounds, will not antagonise the bench and, even if unsuccessful, will have some value in preparing the bench for your closing speech. Even if they are not prepared to stop the case at the close of the prosecution case, the bench may be receptive to similar arguments at a later stage. Always be prepared to address the bench on any point of law necessary to sustain your submission, and when dealing with the law, allude to the clerk, inviting the bench to take his or her advice. Proper deference to the clerk is no less desirable in advocacy in the magistrates' court than to the bench itself.

The defence closing speech is the most potent of forensic weapons in a summary trial. If well prepared, it can have tremendous effect, yet very often, it appears that advocates do no more than say the first things that come into their heads immediately after the flurry of evidence has died down. It is true that time for reflection is short in a summary trial, and that you have to move from one phase of the trial to another with great rapidity. Nonetheless, proper preparation can compensate for much of this. If you have your note of your ideal closing speech, you will add and delete points in the briefest note form, as the evidence emerges. Since you should never write out any speech verbatim, you should have a more than sufficient note of the general order and content of your speech. Taking a note of the evidence is in itself difficult enough, especially when you are on your feet. But again, this can be solved to the extent necessary by leaving a space for the briefest note of the answer opposite your note of your proposed questions.

The content of a closing speech obviously varies widely from case to case, but here again, some guidelines can be established. It is always appropriate to refer briefly to the burden and standard of proof. The bench know perfectly well the principles of law involved, and you should couch your remarks in terms of 'reminding' the court of them. You should also deal with this subject in a few sentences. But is should not be omitted. It makes a good standard opening, during which you can compose and collect yourself a little after the heat of battle. The most recent battleground before your closing speech will often have been your client's evidence, and listening to this can be traumatic for any advocate. Moreover, the burden and standard of proof are vital elements of any criminal trial, and their inclusion at the outset should ensure that everything that follows is seen in that light. Some advocates make a second (extremely brief) mention of it as a concluding observation, and this is often worthwhile in a close case. If the bench are unsure and undecided, the burden and standard of proof are often determinative of the case.

Deal with the law applicable to the case if necessary, bearing in mind that the bench will permit the prosecution to reply on a point of law. Bear in mind the strictures set out in Chapter 9 against reading law reports to those who have no text to follow. In the magistrates' court, reading from law reports is never satisfactory. It is far better to summarise the law for the bench, refer by name to the authorities, and hand them to the clerk for his or her perusal.

When dealing with the facts, it is essential to avoid misstatements of the evidence, and exaggerated statements of the effect of the evidence. With the very best of intentions, this tendency can be difficult to avoid for any enthusiastic advocate. A closing speech sometimes carries its maker away, with the result that his or her memory of the evidence becomes increasingly rose-tinted as time goes on. Any misstatement of the evidence is likely to be picked up by the bench, who have listened to the evidence throughout without the distraction of papers and the conduct of the case. If you catch yourself misstating or exaggerating the evidence, apologise, refer to your notes and get it right. Realism is an essential component of good advocacy in every phase. It can be fatal to say that there is no evidence of something, when your true (and just as cogent) argument is that there is some evidence of it, but that the evidence is plainly insufficient, when judged by reference to the standard of proof. You should always admit the existence of whatever case there may be against you, and then argue against it to the maximum extent possible, rather than trying to bulldoze your way through with specious statements that there is no case against your client. The bench know better. Naked statements that there is no case or no evidence are never as cogent as a balanced, reasoned argument of why the prosecution have failed to discharge the heavy onus of proof which lies upon them in a criminal case.

For the reasons suggested in Chapter 9 in relation to addressing a county court judge, it is always preferable to put a case to a magistrates' court, whether consisting of a lay bench or a stipendiary magistrate, on the basis that the prosecution witnesses are unreliable or mistaken, than on the basis that they have committed perjury or fabricated evidence. This is particularly true when the witnesses concerned are police officers. There is nothing sinister in this. All courts prefer to believe that people are disposed to tell the truth, and it is comforting to all of us to hear that no allegation of improper conduct is being made against the police. The process of persuasion is made easier whenever the tribunal can be reassured on that point. In some cases, you will have no choice but to allege firmly that certain witnesses have been dishonest, but do not assume such a position without good reason.

Finally, bear in mind David Paul Brown's injunction cited in Chapter 9, that the advocate should act as though he is awake, and engaged in a matter of interest to him. Whether or not you believe your client's case is irrelevant; what counts is whether the court find that it has been disproved beyond reasonable doubt. Never even hint that you are a disbeliever. Suspend your disbelief, and be as persuasive as the nature of the case permits.

Appendix
Extracts from Statutes and Rules of Court

Criminal Evidence Act 1898, section 1

1. Every person charged with an offence, and the wife or husband, as the case may be, of the person so charged, shall be a competent witness for the defence at every stage of the proceedings, whether the person so charged is charged solely or jointly with any other person. Provided as follows:—

(a) A person so charged shall not be called as a witness in pursuance of this Act except upon his own application:

(b) The failure of any person charged with an offence, or of the wife or husband, as the case may be, of the person so charged, to give evidence shall not be made the subject of any comment by the prosecution:

(c) The wife or husband of the person charged shall not, save as in this Act mentioned, be called as a witness in pursuance of this Act except upon the application of the person so charged:

(d) Nothing in this Act shall make a husband compellable to disclose any communication made to him by his wife during the marriage, or a wife compellable to disclose any communication made to her by her husband during the marriage:

(e) A person charged and being a witness in pursuance of this Act may be asked any question in cross-examination notwithstanding that it would tend to criminate him as to the offence charged:

(f) A person charged and called as a witness in pursuance of this Act shall not be asked, and if asked shall not be required to answer, any question tending to show that he has committed or been convicted of or been charged with any offence other than that wherewith he is then charged, or is of bad character, unless—

(i)   the proof that he has committed or been convicted of such other offence is admissible evidence to show that he is guilty of the offence wherewith he is then charged; or

(ii)   he has personally or by his advocate asked questions of the witnesses for the prosecution with a view to establish his own good character, or has given evidence of his good character, or the nature or conduct of the defence is such as to involve imputations on the character of the prosecutor or the witnesses for the prosecution; or

(iii)   he has given evidence against any other person charged [in the same proceedings [1]]:

(g)   Every person called as a witness in pursuance of this Act shall, unless otherwise ordered by the court, give his evidence from the witness-box or other place from which the other witnesses give their evidence: [2].

Notes

1. Words substituted by Criminal Evidence Act 1979, s. 1.
2. Paragraph (h) repealed by Criminal Justice Act 1982, s. 78 and sch. 16.

Judges' Rules

These rules do not affect the principles:

(a)   That citizens have a duty to help a police officer to discover and apprehend offenders;

(b)   That police officers, otherwise than by arrest, cannot compel any person against his will to come to or remain in any police station;

(c)   That every person at any stage of an investigation should be able to communicate and to consult privately with a solicitor. This is so even if he is in custody provided that in such a case no unreasonable delay or hindrance is caused to the processes of investigation or the administration of justice by his doing so;

(d)   That when a police officer who is making inquiries of any person about an offence has enough evidence to prefer a charge against that person for the offence, he should without delay cause that person to be charged or informed that he may be prosecuted for the offence;

(e)   That it is a fundamental condition of the admissibility in evidence against any person, equally of any oral answer given by that person to a question put by a police officer and of any statement made by that person, that it shall have been voluntary, in the sense that it has not been obtained from him by fear of prejudice or hope of advantage, exercised or held out by a person in authority, or by oppression.

The principle set out in paragraph (e) above is overriding and applicable in all cases. Within that principle the following rules are put forward as a guide to police officers conducting investigations. Nonconformity with these rules may render answers and statements liable to be excluded from evidence in subsequent criminal proceedings.

Rules

I.   When a police officer is trying to discover whether, or by whom, an offence has been committed he is entitled to question any person, whether suspected or not, from whom he thinks that useful information may be obtained. This is so whether or not the person in question has been taken into custody so long as he has not been charged with the offence or informed that he may be prosecuted for it.

II.   As soon as a police officer has evidence which would afford reasonable grounds for suspecting that a person has committed an offence, he shall caution that person or cause him to be cautioned before putting to him any questions, or further questions, relating to that offence.

The caution shall be in the following terms:

You are not obliged to say anything unless you wish to do so but what you say may be put into writing and given in evidence.

When after being cautioned a person is being questioned, or elects to make a statement, a record shall be kept of the time and place at which any such questioning or statement began and ended and of the persons present.

III.   (a)   Where a person is charged with or informed that he may be prosecuted for an offence he shall be cautioned in the following terms:

Do you wish to say anything? You are not obliged to say anything unless you wish to do so but whatever you say will be taken down in writing and may be given in evidence.

(b)   It is only in exceptional cases that questions relating to the offence should be put to the accused person after he has been charged or informed that he may be prosecuted. Such questions may be put where they are necessary for the purpose of preventing or minimising harm or loss to some other person or to the public or for clearing up an ambiguity in a previous answer or statement.

Before any such questions are put the accused should be cautioned in these terms:

I wish to put some questions to you about the offence with which you have been charged (*or* about the offence for which you may be prosecuted). You are not obliged to answer any of these questions, but if you do the questions and answers will be taken down in writing and may be given in evidence.

Any questions put and answers given relating to the offence must be contemporaneously recorded in full and the record signed by that person or if he refuses by the interrogating officer.

(c)   When such a person is being questioned, or elects to make a statement, a record shall be kept of the time and place at which any questioning or statement began and ended and of the persons present.

IV.   All written statements made after caution shall be taken in the following manner:

(a)   If a person says that he wants to make a statement he shall be told that it is intended to make a written record of what he says. He shall always be asked whether he wishes to write down himself what he wants to say; if he says that he cannot write or that he would like someone to write it for him, a police officer may offer to write the statement for him. If he accepts the offer the police officer shall, before starting, ask the person making the statement to sign, or make his mark to the following:

I, ___wish to make a statement. I want someone to write down what I say. I have been told that I need not say anything unless I wish to do so and that whatever I say may be given in evidence.

(b)   Any person writing his own statement shall be allowed to do so without any prompting as distinct from indicating to him what matters are material.

(c)   The person making the statement, if he is going to write it himself, shall be asked to write out and sign before writing what he wants to say, the following:

I make this statement of my own free will. I have been told that I need not say anything unless I wish to do so and that whatever I say may be given in evidence.

(d)   Whenever a police officer writes the statement, he shall take down the exact words spoken by the person making the statement, without putting any questions other than such as may be needed to make the statement coherent, intelligible and relevant to the material matters; he shall not prompt him.

(e)   When the writing of a statement by a police officer is finished the person making it shall be asked to read it and to make any corrections, alterations or additions he wishes. When he has finished reading it he shall be asked to write and sign or make his mark on the following certificate at the end of the statement:

I have read the above statement and I have been told that I can correct, alter or add anything I wish. This statement is true. I have made it of my own free will.

(f)   If the person who has made a statement refuses to read it or to write the above-mentioned certificate at the end of it or to sign it, the senior police officer present shall record on the statement itself and in the presence of the person making it, what has happened. If the person making the statement cannot read, or refuses to read it, the officer who has taken it down shall read it over to him and ask him whether he would like to correct, alter or add anything and to put his signature or make his mark at the end. The police officer shall then certify on the statement itself what he has done.

V.   If at any time after a person has been charged with, or has been informed that he may be prosecuted for an offence a police officer wishes to bring to the notice of that person any written statement made by another person who in respect of the same offence has also been charged or informed that he may be prosecuted, he shall hand to that person a true copy of such written statement, but nothing shall be said or done to invite any reply or comment. If that person says that he would like to make a statement in reply, or starts to say something, he shall at once be cautioned or further cautioned as prescribed by rule III(a).

VI.   Persons other than police officers charged with the duty of investigating offences or charging offenders shall, so far as may be practicable, comply with these rules.

Criminal Evidence Act 1965, section 1

1.—(1)   In any criminal proceedings where direct oral evidence of a fact would be admissible, any statement contained in a document and tending to establish that fact shall, on production of the document, be admissible as evidence of that fact if—

(a)   the document is, or forms part of, a record relating to any trade or business and compiled, in the course of that trade or business, from information supplied (whether directly or indirectly) by persons who have, or may reasonably be supposed to have, personal knowledge of the matters dealt with in the information they supply; and

(b)   the person who supplied the information recorded in the statement in question is dead, or beyond the seas, or unfit by reason of his bodily or mental condition to attend as a witness, or cannot with reasonable diligence be identified or found, or cannot reasonably be expected (having regard to the time which has elapsed since he supplied the information and to all the circumstances) to have any recollection of the matters dealt with in the information he supplied.

(2)   For the purpose of deciding whether or not a statement is admissible as evidence by virtue of this section, the court may draw any reasonable inference from the form or content of the document in which the statement is contained, and may, in deciding whether or not a person is fit to attend as a witness, act on a certificate purporting

to be a certificate of a fully registered medical practitioner.

(3) In estimating the weight, if any, to be attached to a statement admissible as evidence by virtue of this section regard shall be had to all the circumstances from which any inference can reasonably be drawn as to the accuracy or otherwise of the statement, and, in particular, to the question whether or not the person who supplied the information recorded in the statement did so contemporaneously with the occurrence or existence of the facts stated, and to the question whether or not that person, or any person concerned with making or keeping the record containing the statement, had any incentive to conceal or misrepresent the facts.

(4) In this section 'statement' includes any representation of fact, whether made in words or otherwise, 'document' includes any device by means of which information is recorded or stored and 'business' includes any public transport, public utility or similar undertaking carried on by a local authority and the activities of the Post Office [1].

Note

1. To be construed as including a reference to the British Telecommunications Corporation (British Telecommunications Act 1981, s. 87 and sch. 3, pt 2, para. 42).

Civil Evidence Act 1968, sections 1 to 4

1.—(1) In any civil proceedings a statement other than one made by a person while giving oral evidence in those proceedings shall be admissible as evidence of any fact stated therein to the extent that it is so admissible by virtue of any provision of this Part of this Act or by virtue of any other statutory provision or by agreement of the parties, but not otherwise.

(2) In this section 'statutory provision' means any provision contained in, or in an instrument made under, this or any other Act, including any Act passed after this Act.

2.—(1) In any civil proceedings a statement made, whether orally or in a document or otherwise, by any person, whether called as a witness in those proceedings or not, shall, subject to this section and to rules of court, be admissible as evidence of any fact stated therein of which direct oral evidence by him would be admissible.

(2) Where in any civil proceedings a party desiring to give a statement in evidence by virtue of this section has called or intends to

call as a witness in the proceedings the person by whom the statement was made, the statement—

(a)   shall not be given in evidence by virtue of this section on behalf of that party without the leave of the court; and

(b)   without prejudice to paragraph (a) above, shall not be given in evidence by virtue of this section on behalf of that party before the conclusion of the examination-in-chief of the person by whom it was made, except—

(i)   where before that person is called the court allows evidence of the making of the statement to be given on behalf of that party by some other person; or

(ii)   in so far as the court allows the person by whom the statement was made to narrate it in the course of his examination-in-chief on the ground that to prevent him from doing so would adversely affect the intelligibility of his evidence.

(3)   Where in any civil proceedings a statement which was made otherwise than in a document is admissible by virtue of this section, no evidence other than direct oral evidence by the person who made the statement or any person who heard or otherwise perceived it being made shall be admissible for the purpose of proving it:

Provided that if the statement in question was made by a person while giving oral evidence in some other legal proceedings (whether civil or criminal), it may be proved in any manner authorised by the court.

3.—(1)   Where in any civil proceedings—

(a)   a previous inconsistent or contradictory statement made by a person called as a witness in those procedings is proved by virtue of section 3, 4 or 5 of the Criminal Procedure Act 1865; or

(b)   a previous statement made by a person called as aforesaid is proved for the purpose of rebutting a suggestion that his evidence has been fabricated,

that statement shall by virtue of this subsection be admissible as evidence of any fact stated therein of which direct oral evidence by him would be admissible.

(2)   Nothing in this Act shall affect any of the rules of law relating to the circumstances in which, where a person called as a witness in any civil proceedings is cross-examined on a document used by him to refresh his memory, that document may be made evidence in those proceedings; and where a document or any part of a document is received in evidence in any such proceedings by virtue of any such rule of law, any statement made in that document or part by the person using the document to refresh his memory shall by virtue of this subsection be admissible as evidence of any fact stated therein of which direct oral evidence by him would be admissible.

4.—(1)   Without prejudice to section 5 of this Act, in any civil proceedings a statement contained in a document shall, subject to this section and to rules of court, be admissible as evidence of any fact stated therein of which direct oral evidence would be admissible, if the document is, or forms part of, a record compiled by a person acting under a duty from information which was supplied by a person (whether acting under a duty or not) who had, or may reasonably be supposed to have had, personal knowledge of the matters dealt with in that information and which, if not supplied by that person to the compiler of the record directly, was supplied by him to the compiler of the record indirectly through one or more intermediaries each acting under a duty.

(2)   Where in any civil proceedings a party desiring to give a statement in evidence by virtue of this section has called or intends to call as a witness in the proceedings the person who originally supplied the information from which the record containing the statement was compiled, the statement—

   (a)   shall not be given in evidence by virtue of this section on behalf of that party without the leave of the court; and

   (b)   without prejudice to paragraph (a) above, shall not without the leave of the court be given in evidence by virtue of this section on behalf of that party before the conclusion of the examination-in-chief of the person who originally supplied the said information.

(3)   Any reference in this section to a person acting under a duty includes a reference to a person acting in the course of any trade, business, profession or other occupation in which he is engaged or employed or for the purposes of any paid or unpaid office held by him.

County Court Rules 1981, Order 20, rules 14 to 20

14.—(1) In this Part of this Order [1] 'the Act of 1968' means the Civil Evidence Act 1968 and any expressions used in this Part of this Order and in Part 1 of the Act of 1968 [2] have the same meanings in this Part of this Order as they have in the said Part 1.

(2) This Part of this Order shall apply in relation to the trial or hearing of an issue arising in an action or matter and to a reference under section 93 of the Act [3] as it applies to the trial or hearing of an action or matter.

(3) Nothing in this Part of this Order shall apply to a reference under section 92 of the Act [3].

Notes

1. That is, part 4 of Ord. 20, consisting of rr. 14–26.
2. Part 1 of the Act consists of ss. 1–10.
3. That is, the County Courts Act 1959 (CCR, Ord. 1, r.3).

15.—(1) Subject to the provisions of this rule, a party to an action or matter who desires to give in evidence at the trial or hearing any statement which is admissible in evidence by virtue of section 2, 4 or 5 of the Act of 1968 shall, not less than 14 days before the day fixed for the trial or hearing, give notice of his desire to do so to the registrar and to every other party.

(2) Unless in any particular case the court otherwise directs, paragraph (1) shall not apply to an action or matter in which no defence or answer has been filed; and where a defence or answer is filed less than 14 days before the day fixed for the trial or hearing, any party required to give notice pursuant to paragraph (1) shall apply to the court for an adjournment of the trial or hearing or for such other directions as may be appropriate.

(3) Paragraph (1) shall not apply in relation to any statement which is admissible as evidence of any fact stated therein by virtue not only of the said section 2, 4 or 5 but by virtue also of any other statutory provision within the meaning of section 1 of the Act of 1968.

(4) Paragraph (1) shall not apply in relation to any statement which any party to a probate action desires to give in evidence at the trial of that action and which is alleged to have been made by the deceased person whose estate is the subject of the action.

(5) Where, by virtue of any provision of these rules or of any order

or direction of the court, the evidence in any proceedings is to be given by affidavit then, without prejudice to paragraph (3), paragraph (1) shall not apply in relation to any statement which any party to the proceedings desires to have included in any affidavit to be used on his behalf in the proceedings.

16.   RSC Order 38, rules 22 to 25, shall apply to a notice under the last foregoing rule as they apply to a notice under rule 21 of the said Order 38.

17.—(1)   Subject to paragraphs (2) and (3), any party on whom a notice under rule 15 is served may, within 7 days after service of the notice on him, give to the proper officer and to the party who gave the notice a counter-notice requiring that party to call as a witness at the trial or hearing any person (naming him) particulars of whom are contained in the notice.

(2)   Where any notice under rule 15 contains a statement that any person particulars of whom are contained in the notice cannot or should not be called as a witness for the reason specified therein, a party shall not be entitled to serve a counter-notice under this rule requiring that person to be called as a witness at the trial or hearing unless he contends that that person can or, as the case may be, should be called, and in that case he must include in his counter-notice a statement to that effect.

(3)   Where a statement to which a notice under rule 15 relates is one to which rule 19 applies, no party on whom the notice is served shall be entitled to serve a counter-notice under this rule in relation to that statement, but the foregoing provision is without prejudice to the right of any party to apply to the court under rule 19 for directions with respect to the admissibility of that statement.

(4)   If any party by whom a notice under rule 15 is served fails to comply with a counter-notice duly served on him under this rule, then, unless any of the reasons specified in paragraph (5) applies in relation to the person named in the counter-notice, and without prejudice to the powers of the court under rule 20, the statement to which the notice under rule 15 relates shall not be admissible at the trial or hearing as evidence of any fact stated therein by virtue of section 2, 4 or 5 of the Act of 1968, as the case may be.

(5)   The reasons referred to in paragraph (4) are that the person in question is dead, or beyond the seas, or unfit by reason of his bodily or mental condition to attend as a witness or that despite the exercise of reasonable diligence it has not been possible to identify or find him

or that he cannot reasonably be expected to have any recollection of matters relevant to the accuracy or otherwise of the statement to which the notice relates.

18.—(1) Where a question arises whether any of the reasons specified in rule 17(5) applies in relation to a person particulars of whom are contained in a notice under rule 15, the court may, on the application of any party to the action or matter, determine that question before the trial or hearing or give directions for it to be determined before the trial or hearing and for the manner in which it is to be determined.

(2) Unless the court otherwise directs, notice of any application under paragraph (1) must be served on every other party to the action or matter.

(3) Where any such question as is referred to in paragraph (1) has been determined under or by virtue of that paragraph, no application to have it determined afresh at the trial or hearing may be made unless the evidence which it is sought to adduce in support of the application could not with reasonable diligence have been adduced at the hearing which resulted in the determination.

19.—(1) Where a party has given notice in accordance with rule 15 that he desires to give in evidence at the trial or hearing—

(a) a statement falling within section 2(1) of the Act of 1968 which was made by a person, whether orally or in a document, in the course of giving evidence in some other legal proceedings (whether civil or criminal), or

(b) a statement falling within section 4(1) of the Act of 1968 which is contained in a record of direct oral evidence given in some other legal proceedings (whether civil or criminal),

any party to the action or matter may apply to the court for directions as to whether, and if so on what conditions, the party desiring to give the statement in evidence will be permitted to do so and (where applicable) as to the manner in which that statement and any other evidence given in those other proceedings is to be proved.

20.—(1) Without prejudice to sections 2(2)(a) and 4(2)(a) of the Act of 1968 and rule 19, the court may, if it thinks it just to do so, allow a statement falling within section 2(1), 4(1) or 5(1) of the Act of 1968 to be given in evidence at the trial or hearing of an action or matter notwithstanding—

(a)   that the statement is one in relation to which rule 15(1) applies and that the party desiring to give the statement in evidence has failed to comply with that rule, or

(b)   that that party has failed to comply with any requirement of a counter-notice relating to that statement which was served on him in accordance with rule 17.

(2)   Without prejudice to the generality of paragraph (1), the court may exercise its power under that paragraph to allow a statement to be given in evidence at the trial or hearing if a refusal to exercise that power might oblige the party desiring to give the statement in evidence to call as a witness at the trial or hearing an opposite party or a person who is or was at the material time the servant or agent of an opposite party.

Rules of the Supreme Court 1965, Order 38, rules 22 to 25

These rules were inserted by Rules of the Supreme Court (Amendment) 1969 (SI 1969/1105).

Statement admissible by virtue of section 2 of the Act: contents of notice.
22.—(1)   If the statement is admissible by virtue of section 2 of the Act and was made otherwise than in a document, the notice must contain particulars of—

(a)   the time, place and circumstances at or in which the statement was made;

(b)   the person by whom, and the person to whom, the statement was made; and

(c)   the substance of the statement or, if material, the words used.

(2)   If the statement is admissible by virtue of the said section 2 and was made in a document, a copy or transcript of the document, or of the relevant part thereof, must be annexed to the notice and the notice must contain such (if any) of the particulars mentioned in paragraph (1)(a) and (b) as are not apparent on the face of the document or part.

(3)   If the party giving the notice alleges that any person, particulars of whom are contained in the notice, cannot or should not be called as a witness at the trial or hearing for any of the reasons specified in rule

25, the notice must contain a statement to that effect specifying the reason relied on.

Statement admissible by virtue of section 4 of the Act: contents of notice
23.—(1)   If the statement is admissible by virtue of section 4 of the Act the notice must have annexed to it a copy or transcript of the document containing the statement, or of the relevant part thereof, and must contain—

(a)   particulars of—

(i)   the person by whom the record containing the statement was compiled;

(ii)   the person who originally supplied the information from which the record was compiled; and

(iii)   any other person through whom that information was supplied to the compiler of that record;

and, in the case of any such person as is referred to in (i) or (iii) above, a description of the duty under which that person was acting when compiling that record or supplying information from which that record was compiled, as the case may be;

(b)   if not apparent on the face of the document annexed to the notice, a description of the nature of the record which, or part of which, contains the statement; and

(c)   particulars of the time, place and circumstances at or in which that record or part was compiled.

(2)   If the party giving the notice alleges that any person, particulars of whom are contained in the notice, cannot or should not be called as a witness at the trial or hearing for any of the reasons specified in rule 25, the notice must contain a statement to that effect specifying the reason relied on.

Statement admissible by virtue of section 5 of the Act: contents of notice
24.—(1)   If the statement is contained in a document produced by a computer and is admissible by virtue of section 5 of the Act, the notice must have annexed to it a copy or transcript of the document containing the statement, or of the relevant part thereof, and must contain particulars of—

(a)   a person who occupied a responsible position in relation to the management of the relevant activities for the purposes of which the computer was used regularly during the material period to store or process information;

(b)   a person who at the material time occupied such a position in relation to the supply of information to the computer, being information which is reproduced in the statement or information from which the information contained in the statement is derived;

(c)   a person who occupied such a position in relation to the operation of the computer during the material period;

and where there are two or more persons who fall within any of the foregoing subparagraphs and some only of those persons are at the date of service of the notice capable of being called as witnesses at the trial or hearing, the person particulars of whom are to be contained in the notice must be such one of those persons as is at that date so capable.

(2)   The notice must also state whether the computer was operating properly throughout the material period and, if not, whether any respect in which it was not operating properly or was out of operation during any part of that period was such as to affect the production of the document in which the statement is contained or the accuracy of its contents.

(3)   If the party giving the notice alleges that any person, particulars of whom are contained in the notice, cannot or should not be called as a witness at the trial or hearing for any of the reasons specified in rule 25, the notice must contain a statement to that effect specifying the reason relied on.

Reasons for not calling a person as a witness

25.   The reasons referred to in rules 22(3), 23(2) and 24(3) are that the person in question is dead, or beyond the seas, or unfit by reason of his bodily or mental condition to attend as a witness or that despite the exercise of reasonable diligence it has not been possible to identify or find him or that he cannot reasonably be expected to have any recollection of matters relevant to the accuracy or otherwise of the statement to which the notice relates.

County Court Rules 1981, Order 20, rules 27 and 28

27.—(1)   Except with the leave of the court or where all parties agree, no expert evidence may be adduced at the trial or hearing of an action or matter, unless the party seeking to adduce the evidence has applied to the court to determine whether a direction should be given under rule 37, 38 or 41 (whichever is appropriate) of RSC Order 38, as applied by rule 28 of this Order, and has complied with any direction given on the application.

(2)   Nothing in paragraph (1) shall apply to expert evidence which is permitted to be given by affidavit or which is to be adduced in an action or matter in which no defence or answer has been filed or in proceedings referred to arbitration under section 92 of the Act [1].

(3)   Nothing in paragraph (1) shall affect the enforcement under any other provision of these rules (except Order 29, rule 1) of a direction given under this Part of this Order.

Note
1.   That is, the County Courts Act 1959 (CCR, Ord. 1, r. 3).

28.   RSC Order 38, rules 37 to 44, shall apply in relation to an application under rule 27 of this Order as they apply in relation to an application under rule 36(1) of the said Order 38.

Rules of the Supreme Court 1965, Order 38, rules 37 to 44

These rules were added by Rules of the Supreme Court (Amendment) 1974 (SI 1974/295) and a new rule 37 and new title for rule 38 were substituted by Rules of the Supreme Court (Amendment No. 2) 1980 (SI 1980/1010) which also revoked rule 40.

Expert evidence in actions for personal injuries
37.—(1)   This rule applies to any action for personal injuries, except—

(a)   any Admiralty action; and

(b)   any action where the pleadings contain an allegation of a negligent act or omission in the course of medical treatment.

(2)   Where an application is made under rule 36(1) in respect of oral expert evidence, then, unless the Court considers that there is

sufficient reason for not doing so, it shall direct that the substance of the evidence be disclosed in the form of a written report or reports to such other parties and within such period as the Court may specify.

(3)   Where the expert evidence relates to medical matters the Court may, if it thinks fit, treat the following circumstances as sufficient reason for not giving a direction under paragraph (2), namely that the expert evidence may contain an expression of opinion—

(i)   as to the manner in which the personal injuries were sustained; or

(ii)   as to the genuineness of the symptoms of which complaint is made.

(4)   Where the expert evidence does not relate to medical matters, the Court may, if it thinks fit, treat as a sufficient reason for not giving a direction under paragraph (2) any of the circumstances set out in sub-paragraphs (a) or (b) of rule 38(2).

Expert evidence in other actions

38.—(1)   Where an application is made under rule 36(1) in respect of oral expert evidence to which rule 37 does not apply, the Court may, if satisfied that it is desirable to do so, direct that the substance of any expert evidence which is to be adduced by any party be disclosed in the form of a written report or reports to such other parties and within such period as the Court may specify.

(2)   In deciding whether to give a direction under paragraph (1) the Court shall have regard to all the circumstances and may, to such extent as it thinks fit, treat any of the following circumstances as affording a sufficient reason for not giving such a direction:—

(a)   that the expert evidence is or will be based to any material extent upon a version of the facts in dispute between the parties; or

(b)   that the expert evidence is or will be based to any material extent upon facts which are neither—

(i)   ascertainable by the expert by the exercise of his own powers of observation, nor

(ii)   within his general professional knowledge and experience.

Disclosure of part of expert evidence

39.   Where the Court considers that any circumstances rendering it undesirable to give a direction under rule 37 or 38 relate to part only of the evidence sought to be adduced, the Court may, if it thinks fit, direct disclosure of the remainder.

Expert evidence contained in statement
41.   Where an application is made under rule 36 in respect of expert evidence contained in a statement and the applicant alleges that the maker of the statement cannot or should not be called as a witness, the Court may direct that the provisions of rules 20 to 23 and 25 to 33 shall apply with such modifications as the Court thinks fit.

Putting in evidence expert report disclosed by another party
42.   A party to any cause or matter may put in evidence any expert report disclosed to him by any other party in accordance with this Part of this Order.

Time for putting expert report in evidence
43.   Where a party to any cause or matter calls as a witness the maker of a report which has been disclosed . . . [1] in accordance with a direction given under rule 37 or 38, the report may be put in evidence at the commencement of its maker's examination-in-chief or at such other time as the Court may direct.

Note
1.   Words deleted by Rules of the Supreme Court (Amendment No. 2) 1982 (SI 1982/1111).

Revocation and variation of directions
44.   Any direction given under this Part of this Order may on sufficient cause being shown be revoked or varied by a subsequent direction given at or before the trial of the cause or matter.

Index